RESILIENT

ACHIEVING THE AMERICAN DREAM

A MEMOIR BY
LENNY BAZEMORE

Published by Bazemore Publishing LLC, Los Angeles, California

Paperback- ISBN: 979-8-9890707-0-1

Hardcover- ISBN: 979-8-9890707-1-8

ebook- ISBN: 979-8-9890707-2-5

Audiobook- ISBN:979-8-9890707-3-2

www.LennyBazemore.com

Contents

Forward

TERESA BRYCE BAZEMORE

How do you describe someone who is indescribable, someone who lights up a room whenever he is in it? How do you describe someone who is resilient through many trials and tribulations, but yet is able to maintain a heart of gold?

It was my sixth day in Philadelphia and I decided it was time to check out the best two gyms to keep up with my most recent fitness commitment. One was just a block from my office so I decided to start there. How would I know that I was about to meet the man who would become my life partner? You know that God has his hand in things when the circumstances come together as they did. Lenny wasn't even working at the time, just working out, but graciously agreed to show "the nice lady", according to the front desk greeter, around the facility. He was so engaging and friendly that we easily fell into not only a tour but a conversation about Philadelphia, music and my move to the city.

Despite his great salesmanship, I told him that I'd have to check out the other gym before making a decision. Nevertheless, he offered to be a resource to me since I was new to the area. He called me the next day to check in and even after I decided to join the other gym, he continued to touch base with me to see how I was doing. Over the next few months, our friendship blossomed first by phone and email and then getting together for a bite to eat. Our conversations were easy, interesting and comfortable as we talked about all kinds of subjects.

So you can imagine my surprise, when he told me he didn't have a college degree. Here was this guy who was so intelligent and knowledgeable about such a wide array of subjects. In fact, he was smarter than many of the college graduates I knew. How could that be? See, I grew up in a middle-class black neighborhood in Virginia where almost everyone went to college. It was just expected. I then learned about his story which unfortunately is how so many wonderful and intelligent young black men get derailed in life. Fortunately, as you will read, Lenny didn't allow those setbacks to permanently derail him.

Getting to know Lenny was like peeling back the layers of an onion. As we spent more time together, I learned more about the many challenges he had growing up and I was so impressed with his grit and determination. I also was taken with his positive attitude and quest for continual learning and self-improvement. We always laugh about the fact that he always seems to know something about a lot of things.

He really is a renaissance man. I've seen him solve engineering problems that others were stumped on how to solve. At the same time, he can produce a beautiful painting or create beautiful designs and special touches for his real estate projects. We share and enjoy a wide variety of interests from attending Las Vegas Raiders games to attending shows on Broadway or taking in a new art exhibit. And of course, travel is a passion we both share. I'm not sure that I would have gone to Antarctica without his enthusiasm and encouragement.

One of the things that impressed me and that I love most about him is his commitment to his kids, Jordan, Alexis and Devon. The first time I was driving them somewhere, I received a lecture on how special and important they are and that I had to drive carefully. Of course, I quickly reminded him that I had been driving longer than he had. He also consistently demonstrates the same commitment to his Mom, his niece and her family.

Another passion we both share is helping others. Over the years, I have seen Lenny reach out to assist others with a genuine interest in helping them find their best path to success. He was the driving force behind our donations to Habitat for Humanity of Montgomery County, Pa. and has been a consistent and ardent supporter of Rush Arts Philadelphia and Where Art Can Occur (WACO Theater in North Hollywood). Both of these charities make an important and lasting difference in the lives of young people. Especially after the significant challenges he has experienced, he knows the value of helping kids understand that each and every person has gifts and the ability to succeed no matter the adversity they have experienced.

I have been privileged to experience his love and support for more than 13 years of marriage and almost 17 years of knowing each other. I know that he will always be there for me. When I was managing a company through the Great Financial Crisis, he was always there to listen to me, offer advice, go for a walk or just sit and chat over a glass of wine. I couldn't ask for a better life partner. He pushes me to be the best that I can be as well. I'm so grateful that Lenny was able to meet and get to know my father. My father was a special person that everyone young and old admired and adored, especially me, so when he told me that he thought that Lenny was a "good guy" that meant a lot, not that I hadn't already figured it out for myself.

Lenny Bazemore is not only resilient, he is the love of my life and my best friend!

Preface

On several occasions after hearing me tell a few stories over the years, people mentioned that I should write a book about my life. It's filled with interesting anecdotes that shaped the person that I am and as I looked back on it all, I came to the realization that my story is not all that unique. There are countless people in the world who have endured equally difficult lives and in many cases much worse than mine and my heart goes out to them. For me, this was a monumental feat and I feel blessed to have accomplished it. I believe some people will relate to my book and others may be inspired. I spent 2 years working on it and in the beginning, I experienced horrible flashbacks that led to severe anxiety attacks. I sought therapy because I needed professional help in dealing with those powerful emotions. I opened Pandora's box and left the lid open searching for "Hope" at the bottom of it. The amount of work I had to put in just to heal from the PTSD was immense and I did not set out to create this book to share with the public. I wrote this book to personally heal and move past my years of depression and trauma. Many of my family and friends do not know this information and I wanted to share it with them so they could know me better. After my memoir was complete, I decided that I would also like to share it with the world in hopes that it may help someone understand that dark days don't last forever because there will always be light at the end of the tunnel. You just have to keep fighting and moving forward.

I have a few tattoos on my body that have deep personal meaning. They translate to being resilient and are based on the "Legend of the Koi fish and the Waterfall," from beautiful Asian culture. The story is about Koi swimming upstream against the powerful current for a hundred years. Some turned back because it was too challenging. For the ones who continued, the reward was in the journey to learn how to persevere through difficult times. They swam upstream until they reached the waterfall. Many tried to jump to the top but most of them gave up and swam back down stream to an easier life. One day, a very special Koi realized that if he swam down to where it was the darkest and deepest, he would be able to increase his upward momentum. Up and up he swam gaining speed and power. He gave it everything he had as he jumped out of the water landing at the top of the waterfall. He was rewarded for his resilience, intelligence and fortitude by being turned into a Golden Dragon. Another one of my nicknames is "The Golden Dragon" because I identify with that one particular Koi who made it through in spite of the difficulties in life.

ZenLen

Invitation

Hello, my name is Lenny Bazemore and I would like to invite you into my world. In this memoir, I want to share with you some of the highly memorable events throughout my life. There is so much more to it all but I narrowed it down just in case we decide to make it into a movie. These stories are the more significant parts of my experiences. I am fortunate to be able to live and write about an extremely eventful life and survive it all. Thank you for reading and I appreciate your support.

P.S. I assure you, this book was written by me, a real human, and not AI.

ONE

My Introduction to Healing

In 1992, This dude named Lark Ramsey had just clocked me in the jaw. I punched him back with a quick combination, a left then a right. I grabbed him and slammed his head against the wall then body slammed him onto the blacktop of the parking lot. I started punching him and soon after, I felt two quick hits on my back. I reached around and touched my shirt. I felt something warm and wet. It was blood. No fucking way was I just stabbed twice. I touched the blood again, this time to make sure it was real, but I could feel myself slipping out of consciousness as I fell over. Everything looked so...out of focus. The faces I could still see, the fists launching into my body I could feel. Everything had a blurriness to it. People were screaming, and he was attacking me. I felt helpless, scared and afraid to die. The darkness was turning to light, and blood was gushing everywhere.

It was now 2022, 30 years later and I remember waking up screaming "I don't want to die" over and over again, the bedsheets trapped around my legs, the darkness of the bedroom suffocating me.

It must have woken Teresa because I remember seeing her beautiful, yet worried face, trying to calm me down.

But she couldn't. Something wasn't right. My chest was tight, I struggled to breathe, and it felt like someone was smothering me.

Teresa called 911 at 3:30 in the morning and I tried to calm down. I know we must all die at some point but all I could think about was—everything we worked for. There I was, just a little black kid from Norristown who fought his way out of poverty to become the first millionaire in his family. Living in a beautiful $10 million dollar home in the Hollywood Hills overlooking all of Los Angeles with his and hers Bentleys. Our charitable contributions that help so many other people, the international vacations— What the fuck is going on, I thought. This can't be happening in my life right now, I have so much left to do. The way I see it, I'm just getting started in life!

This claustrophobic smothering feeling happened once before —on a flight to LA while leaving Las Vegas after watching my Raiders play. I was able to breathe my way out of it. But this time, it felt more lethal somehow.

When the EMTs arrived, they told me that my vitals looked fine. Probably just stress, they said, no doubt looking around at our home and assuming that riches don't always come easy.

I scheduled an appointment with a therapist, Dr. Kelly, which wasn't easy for me. You see, therapy isn't as prevalent in black households. Oftentimes there's a fear of judgment. I started to wonder, "Am I weak or something?"

I don't know, maybe I was just being too damn stubborn but I had to move forward, because I was having panic attacks and I do not like feeling out of control.

I jumped on the highway and headed to my first appointment. On the way there, I started hyperventilating while driving and had to pull over. I used the breathing technique again to calm me down. I started to feel better and after another 15 minutes of driving, I pulled into the parking lot and strolled into her office building. Dr. Kelly met me at the door and walked me into her office. I sat on the couch and she sat across from me in a chair next to the little table with a lamp on it. She was a confident woman. She was kind, intelligent, and professional.

She asked what brought me to schedule a session with her. Unsure of where to start, I told her, "Some people say I talk about money too much and that I cuss too much."

Mostly, I wanted to make her laugh to break the ice and make the whole thing feel a little less formal. I had gone to therapy a few times before, each time a bust. But there was something different about Dr. Kelly, something welcoming. I felt like I could trust her immediately. But, I was still a little unsure. What if she tells me that she can't help me or there was no hope of being so-called fixed, I wondered. But still, I continued.

"While you're in a session with me," she said, "you can say whatever the fuck you want."

She asked about my relationship with money, so I told her I was from a small town just outside of Philly, called Norristown where none of us grew up with any real family money. No one ever taught us the true power or value of it," I said. "In certain situations, sure I talk about money—because I use it as a technique to manifest more of it. I am not afraid of its power and I know its value. Besides, I also like to share my opinion with other people on how it works. I understand that someone may feel uncomfortable talking about money because of their lack of knowledge about it. Some people just see money as a tool to pay off bills or buy things, and in some of those situations, they buy depreciating assets to fill an emotional void, trying to make themselves feel better. You know, instant gratification. Where I grew up, you would see a few guys wear top designer clothes and drive around in expensive cars. They were always trying to impress people and spend their money on things that don't matter instead of investing it for their future. Also, they just happened to still live at home with their parents or lived in a tiny apartment. I just don't like to see people waste money on things that don't matter. I would rather see them use their money as an investment tool because money makes money faster than most humans make money. I deserve the quality of life that my wife and I have earned and I'm really just sharing information. Some people enjoy hobbies like fishing and candle making. One of my hobbies is making money to ensure a quality of life on earth. Whether you grow up rich or poor, there is no real understanding of money when you are young. Either way, rich or poor, you have to be taught about it. But for me and my friends, we didn't have anyone around to teach us. We didn't fully understand that we were poor and there was a beautiful innocence about that. Then you get a little older, those feelings of sadness and confusion about the haves and have nots start to set in. And when I was a kid, I experienced what it was like to do without and I didn't want to be a have not anymore. I just wanted to make something of myself, to help my family get out of poverty, and to never have to worry about money again."

I don't remember exactly what it was, but somewhere in between my panic attacks and money, she said something that made me crack wide open. Maybe the stories of my past were held in for too long or maybe she was sent by God. Either way, I found myself telling her everything.

"Do you recall your earliest memory?" she asked.

"Yeah. I was the first grandkid to live with my grandparents on Washington Street. I was a speedy little guy, and my grand-mother used to tell me all the time to stop running in the house." "You're going to hit your head on the coffee table," She would shout. She also would say that I was hard headed. "Well one day I didn't stop and bam—my head met the corner of that coffee table right quick. They rushed me to the hospital and stitched me up. A major concussion at two years old and I still have the little scar right between my eyes. Here," I said, pointing to my forehead.

"That was the first of many near-death experiences. I've been through some shit and I'm lucky to be alive. I try to live in a constant state of gratitude because of what I've been through," I said.

I told her about the time my older cousin Nimmy taught me

how to fight when I was just four years old. I told her a story about the time a little boy's older brother nearly killed me with a shard of glass to the forehead. The time I was almost run over—twice, and the time I was stabbed—twice and had a gun pointed at my head. How I was falsely accused of assault, which led to my college football scholarship—which was my one-way ticket out of poverty—being revoked, and everything in between. I told her about my fucked up father situation. Technically I had two dads, but it never felt that way, given that my biological father was absent for all of my childhood, and when I finally did meet him, he turned out to be void of any and all emotion. My stepfather, on the other hand, was a drunk who lived in the same house as me but never took the time to speak to me or share whatever wisdom he possessed. It was like living with a stranger.

"Do you think about these things a lot?" Dr. Kelly asked.

"Well," I said, "I'm writing a book about my life."

"How's that going?"

"It's good. Tough but good," I said. "Actually, it's really tough. I'll hype myself up, ready to write, get a few paragraphs in, and then I stop."

Dr. Kelly wondered if my panic attacks and writer's block might be caused by all of the trauma I've been through—the near-death experiences, the poverty, the lack of any real father figure.

"You may be experiencing some PTSD. There is no doubt that you are tough," she said. "And look at what you've achieved in America as a black man from Norristown. I'm sure that can take its toll."

But I didn't see it that way. Sure, I showed signs of depression throughout my life, but I did what most black people do—I fixed what I could, and then I moved on. Where I come from we say we put the rest in God's hands. Anyway, I just put it behind me. I've had successes and failures in my life repeatedly but I just never gave up. I am a survivor and a solution based thinker. I am resilient.

But then, I wondered, why was I having panic attacks if I was good to go? I already achieved my dreams, goals and ambitions and needed to create new ones. Why is it that all of a sudden, I am having a tough time suppressing my emotions? I used to be able to push them to the side and move on through any and all trauma.

TWO

Stronger than a Condom

Let me paint you a picture. It was the summer of love—1968. Nearing the end of the decade—a country with new intentions of invigorating citizens to dream bigger, brighter, and better, and to actually do better, to become successful, to fully embrace the curated American Dream.

Gender equality added fresh new colors to the dynamic. Protests raged against the Vietnam War, with students at Howard University embracing Afrocentrism and black unity, inciting a new epoch of student activism while American soldiers murdered as many as 500 unarmed civilians at My Lai, and raped dozens of women and children. And American white supremacy's gang of merry motherfuckers dealt a massive blow to the leaders of the Civil Rights movement, brutally assassinating Martin Luther King, Jr., in Memphis and, just two months later shooting Senator Robert F. Kennedy after a speech in Los Angeles where he died the next day.

NASA's Apollo 8 orbited the moon, making it the first time a crewed spacecraft left the low orbit of Earth. An amazing feat in history and also paving the way for Apollo 11 to do the same but then taking it a step further by landing on the moon, allowing Commander Neil Armstrong to be the first person to walk on the surface. Boeing introduced the very first jumbo jet, changing transportation across the skies as we knew it. And most importantly, the Civil Rights Act of 1968 was signed by President Johnson.

Everything positive and good that happened that year culminated in a melting pot labeled "The American Dream," which was more alive than ever.

But only some of that mattered in Norristown, Pennsylvania.

Located about thirty minutes west of Philadelphia. Norristown was in a world all its own. By which I mean, most people who are born there focus on making a better life for themselves where they live instead of moving elsewhere. It's true that a small percentage of people leave, but it's not easy. For those who do get out, they will always hold Norristown in their hearts. I think most folks from Norristown have a desire and hope of achieving the American Dream, but only some have accomplished that goal in the way that outsiders define it. Mostly because it wasn't as equitable as we've all been taught to believe. In order to obtain that dream, especially if you were black like me, one had to look outside of Norristown to find better opportunities to create financial stability.

Certainly, there was growth within Norristown, but to get out of there, good luck kid. Make no mistake about it though: the people of Norristown are tough. They're strong. They're proud and smart. They know they're just as good as any outsider and they don't need your validation. We just had to redefine what it means to achieve the American Dream. For most of us, It simply means being proud of who you are and where you come from. It also means surviving in this world through any and all situations. If you put someone from Norristown on the Survivor TV show, they win all day every day!

Folks from there have to fight a little harder, fight a little longer, and they always wear their heart on their sleeve.

Especially back then, in the summer of love.

The beginning of the summer in 68, Norristown High was just closing out the school year with its annual prom. Everyone was trying to figure out who they'd ask, which beau was worthy of their hand, which young lady they thought they could snag. (Let's be real, these were teenagers.) And right there in the heart of all that heat was Ms. Gwen Tuggle.

Gwen's family had migrated from Monroe, Georgia, in Walton County when she was just 2 years old. Soon after they moved, she and her twin brother Lenton, were playing in the family's car when it caught on fire almost killing them both. Thank God they were saved and only suffered a few burns. Lenton had a tough time rehabilitating but Gwen was fine. Her dad was a factory worker and handyman, and mom was a house-wife and sometimes cleaned the neighbor's home. Monroe wasn't exactly known for being a hospitable incubator for its black citizens at that time, and they figured they had a better chance of making more money and raising a family up north than they did in the South. Everyone always talked about the American Dream this, and the American Dream that, but no one ever mentioned the caveat "for whites only."

All I think the Tuggle's really wanted was hope – hope that their daughter and other children would finally have a chance to make it in this country. Really, all they wanted was to escape the disgustingly brutal stranglehold racist white culture in the South had on them. Why stick around and give them their souls? Hell no. That wasn't the Tuggle family way. They packed up their belongings and hit the road, heading north to Norristown, Penn-sylvania.

They found a house on W. Washington Street, a block from the Schuylkill River. And there they replanted their roots, in hopes of raising a family, in hopes of bettering their opportunities, in hopes of having a piece of the American Dream—whatever that could have even looked like for black folks back then.

Sixteen years after that move, class at Norristown High had just ended and all the kids were coming and going. Down at the end of the crowded hall, a star athlete on the track team named Hampton Coleman Jr, had his eyes on Gwen. He spoke with Gwen before and thought of taking her out a few times, but otherwise, they never really had a connection. All I know is that they must have shared the same energy on some level because Gwen said yes to the prom and afterwards, they went down to the Schuylkill River. It was a quiet little hideaway with just enough privacy so they could sweet talk, romance, and of course, do what some teenagers do on prom night. I don't have to spell it out for you, do I?

At the end of the night, when Hampton drove Gwen back to her parents' home, she jumped out of the car and headed toward the house, but before she reached the front door, she stopped, turned around, marched back to the car, and said, "And I *better not be pregnant either.*"

I'd bet a million dollars on the fact that Hampton probably scoffed at this.

"She's crazy," He probably said to himself, rolling his eyes. He hardly knew her like that, and there was no way she could be pregnant because he used a condom.

But what he overlooked was they were in Norristown—home of the people that are used to fighting for their lives.

There's this old southern superstition where if you dream about fish, that means someone in your proximity is pregnant.

Well, when Gwen's aunt, who came to town later that month from Georgia, announced to the dinner table that she had a dream about fish, you better believe everyone's eyes darted around that table.

"Well, it ain't me!" Gwen said with the verbal equivalent of putting her foot down.

But deep down, she knew it was her. A million thoughts

flooded her mind, thoughts like, I'm too young to be a mom, I hardly know that fool, and he used a condom anyway.

That he did. But it didn't change anything. You see, the child conceived that night down by the water was me, Leonard Arnett Bazemore, a Pisces born in February. And ever since the beginning, not even a condom could stop me because I was a fighter. Born to be tough. To be bold. To be self-sufficient. Reliable and **RESILIENT**.

THREE

Grandparents, Gwen, and Me

Keep your dress tail down and your legs crossed. And if you don't, you will be the dishonorable leaf on your family tree, a disgrace for all the world to see.

That's about the extent of sex education taught to young girls back in the day to scare them into celibacy. There was no talk of how the body worked or how easy it was to get pregnant. No one talked about how being a mother will change your life forever. There was this unspoken notion that if you got pregnant as a young, unwed lady, you'd bring embarrassment to your family and lose your parents respect. So much so that there were many families that would, if their unmarried daughters got pregnant, send her down South to give birth, give the baby up for adoption or let another family member raise it, and then return the young mother home to continue with her life.

Gwen was petrified to tell her parents she was pregnant. She sat up in her bedroom searching for the courage to call her parents to her room.

Each time she tried to shout "mom," it would come out a whisper.

After several attempts, she figured her mom must not have heard her and so, she'd try again tomorrow.

Then one day when she got to work, she finally found the courage. She called home and, through petrifying nervousness, said to her mom, "Can you tell Dad I'm pregnant, and if he doesn't want me there, I'll leave." Her mother was understandably upset but showed my mom grace and compassion.

She had no clue where she would go, but she knew the values some families held, and she was prepared to deal with the consequences.

Her two older sisters before her had gotten pregnant, but the difference was that they married their partners in crime. Gwen had no intention of marrying Hampton. She told me that nobody was going to make her do something she didn't want to do.

A few months prior to her soiree with Hampton down by the river, Gwen had taken the aptitude test to become a nurse and passed. Back then, if you were a woman and exceptionally intelligent, you may have been able to go to a few colleges. Most women could choose to be either stay at home wives or moms, secretaries, nurses, teachers, or another occupation that wafts hints of sexism. With the Tuggle's financial situation, she couldn't afford nursing school, so she went down to Bell Telephone on Cherry Street and got a job as a telephone operator.

Gwen was one of the better operators, taking pride in her work and never missing a beat. She would spend her long, often tiring shifts in line at the switchboard answering and relaying calls.

Over the intercom speaker one day, an announcement said, "Gwen Tuggle, step out of line, Gwen Tuggle, step out of line." Step out of line was a phrase you usually didn't want to hear. She removed her headset and headed for the manager's office, acutely aware of the baby growing in her belly.

Before the door even closed, her boss said, "Why didn't you tell us you were pregnant when we hired you?"

Without skipping a beat, Gwen replied, with a touch of attitude, "I didn't think it was any of your business."

Now, let me set you straight on a few things here. In this country, in 1968, especially when you're a young black woman, you didn't talk back to authority like that. You don't question authority, you don't disrespect authority, and you certainly don't put yourself in the crosshairs. You say yes ma'am and no ma'am, no sir and yes sir! Disrespect could be detrimental. Remember, this was just a few months after President Johnson signed into law the Civil Rights Act of 1968. Martin Luther King, Jr., had just been assassinated and racial tensions were at their highest. Funny how some things seem to never change. For an 18 year-old pregnant girl to talk back to her boss—no matter her race—now that's just playing with fire.

When my mom tells me this story now, it evokes a metaphorical "amen" and serves as a staunch reminder that you don't tell my mom what to do.

But when it came to her father, Chester Tuggle, that was a different story. He was incensed by Gwen's pregnancy. Had he not told her to keep her dress tail down? Had he not explained what an embarrassment it would be to the family, the family that had moved up north to escape the pitfalls of the lower-class establishment? In retrospect, it had nothing to do with her getting pregnant, but everything to do with his confidence in his fatherhood. Was he not a good dad? Did he not put in enough effort or love? He thought he had tried his hardest, but what if he hadn't?

He made it clear that Gwen wasn't welcome in his home, and so, she sought refuge at her sister Ann's house. And there for a while, not a thought was to be had about Gwen and that child in her belly.

I don't know what really happened in my grandfather's mind, but I like to imagine that he found an answer to all those questions, and deep in his heart he knew that he was, in fact, a good father. The whole reason he had moved the family to Norristown was so they—in particular, Gwen—could have a better life and a chance at being successful—hopefully, inching just a step closer to the American Dream.

And so, after a few months, he told Gwen she could come

back home. Under one condition, of course: that she keeps her dress tail down and her legs *crossed*.

And thankfully so, because on February 22, 1969, at Sacred Heart Hospital, I pushed my way into the world at 7 pounds, 11 ounces and was welcomed into my grandparents' home—a place that would become my refuge for almost two decades, an incubator that would position me to become the first millionaire in my family, but not before my entire life came crumbling down around me—repeatedly.

Despite being one of many grandchildren in the family, I was the first of us to live in the home on W. Washington Street, making me a fan favorite with my grandma. We lived with Mom Mom and Pop Pop until I was about two years old because my mom couldn't afford a place of her own. And the best part of it, there were always people around—friends and family. It was a hub that naturally attracted community and love. When my mom would go to work at Bell Telephone, Mom Mom would take care of me, whipping up her famous PB&Js and teaching me all she knew about the world.

Like I said, I was conceived in Norristown—I busted through the barrier of life—and I was ready to persevere. By the time I was two years old, I was running through my Mom Mom's house like a bat out of hell. Even then I like to think that I had a need for speed in life, that it gave me a desire to live as much as I could. Man, I would dart left and then dart right and every time Mom Mom would say, "Stop running in the house!" She'd warn me about what would happen and call me hard headed when I wouldn't heed the warning. But I could hardly hear her. How could I with all that adrenaline coursing through me? Each time, I'd slow down, but only to catch my breath.

But all this I don't remember. This is what they told me. What I do remember, though—my very first memory—was charging through the house just fast enough that I tripped, just like Mom

Mom said I would, and hit my head on the corner of the coffee table. They rushed me to the hospital and stitched me up, and I'm sure there was a PB&J waiting for me when we made it back home. I never thought about running through that house again, and to this day, right there between my eyes on my forehead is a small scar, a reminder, not of the dangers of rushing through life or heeding my grandma's warnings, but rather a reminder of my passion for living. And every time I look at that scar in the mirror, I remember my dear grandmother, my protector, my heart. You see, she and my mother were the ones who taught me love and grace.

Through this story you're going to hear about some of the men who did me wrong in my life. But some of the women in my life, the women like my mom and my grandma—they are the real heroes of this story. Please don't ever forget about them.

I was Mom Mom's little errand boy. Whatever she needed, I'd run out to get it. You know she was a true southerner through and through because of the C.C. she'd chew (for you city slickers, C.C. is a form of chewing tobacco), complete with a spit can and everything. But Mom Mom was a hardworking woman, and I know for certain her work ethic was one of the greatest influences on me. She used to clean this white lady's house just a few houses up from ours, you know, cleaning dishes, washing the laundry, the typical duties. The woman used to give me candy every time I'd visit, and you know I'd be all over it, excited to stop by and get my little treat. What's interesting, though, is that all of the houses on our block were about the same size, but there was something about this lady's house that made it look so much bigger than ours, so when I would visit my Mom Mom while she was working, I'd sit in awe of this "mansion." Looking back, who knows why I thought it was so much bigger. Maybe it was because they could afford a cleaning lady who also cleaned our house in her spare time.

My grandfather, on the other hand, instilled a lot of foundational tools in me. He was one of the men in my life that never let me down.

Pop Pop worked in a factory and around the time I was four, he started his own restaurant and had it for a short while, but my uncles kept stealing the money in the register which put him out of business. One of my favorite things about my Pop Pop, though, was that he had many gardens that he secretly planted behind a bunch of commercial buildings all around Norristown, and he used to take me out on little adventures, putting me in his Chevy truck and driving around to harvest his crop. I specifically remember one garden behind the PennDOT drivers' testing center at the intersection of Swede Road and Norris City Avenue. After we collected the tomatoes, cabbage, squash and cucumbers, we would head home then he'd take me by the hand down to the Schuylkill River to go fishing. I'd sit there and watch him catch fish; God knows how close we were to where I was conceived.

After the catfish were caught and the sun was starting to set, we'd walk back to the house, and he would send me through the door holding the goods as if I had caught the fish. Sometimes dragging them a little because of the weight. And that meant the world to me—not that my grandmother thought I did all the hard work, but that a man in my life cared enough to spend time with me. Mom Mom would take the vegetables and fish and cook up a storm that lasted for days. My Pop pop taught me lessons on having good behavior, treating people with respect, making something out of very little and the importance of providing for your family.

You see, like I said before, a couple of the men in my life failed to rise to the occasion. But not my Pop Pop. Taking a kid to harvest some vegetables and hook some catfish may not seem like a big deal to some, but comparatively speaking, Pop Pop was everything to me.

In 1971, around the time I was two years old, my Aunt Jeanie took me to see my mom who was hard at work down at the phone company. I remember standing in front of her building getting ready to go in. A man, carrying a basket full of toys, was standing next to a car parked on the corner at Cherry and W. Penn Streets. And next thing I remember, he was gone. Many years later, I asked my Aunt Jeanie who that man was and why did he have all those toys? As it turns out, that was Hampton Coleman Jr.—my biological father. But if he could bring me toys, why couldn't he stay? Why wasn't he in my life?

My mother had applied for child support, but because of her rigid schedule and superlative work ethic down at Bell, she said she forgot about the hearing. The case was thrown out and my mom never saw a dime or reapplied for support. Money that surely would have helped our household.

Eventually my mom did marry a guy we all called JB—short for James Frank Bazemore. It must have been around this time that my last name was changed from Tuggle to Bazemore and when Hampton dropped the toys off to my Aunt Jeanie at Bell, that my mom told Hampton that he couldn't come around anymore because JB didn't want him in the picture. And just like that, he was gone.

Hampton didn't fight for me either. He helped to bring a kid into this world and turned his back on me. He didn't attempt to have any contact with me for another 12 years.

I didn't even know JB was my stepfather until I was finishing eighth grade. But my soul—a child's soul—felt the absence of my real dad. And what Hampton left me with for a father—JB—was nothing more than a cowardly slap in the face to a two-year-old with a scar between his eyes.

FOUR

Red is the Color of Blood

Because my mom and JB married when I was around two, I operated under the belief that I was the result of my mom and JB —a mother and a father. I believed that he and I shared the same DNA, the same ancestors, the same ways of being, that I was a product of him, a result of him. And when you believe you are the product of a man who was seemingly useless as a father and a husband, it really fucks with you mentally when he is so distant from everything and everyone.

You see, JB contributed very little to my childhood, if anything at all. He barely ever spoke to me growing up. Living in the same house with him was awkward for my entire life. He was no better than any stranger I could pull off the street to be my father figure. JB was a fan of his alcohol though; his image never seemed complete without a drink in one hand and a cigarette in the other. And he had this weird, narcissistic obsession with putting his initials on everything he owned in the house. I wasn't even allowed to touch his precious train set in the basement that he seemed to love more than me.

By the time I was conscious in this world, he was already three sheets to the wind. It was rare to see him not drunk or, at a minimum, in the pursuit of drinking. When he'd get home from work, often wearing an army hat, jeans, and polished combat boots, he'd request a cocktail from me—his child bartender. With a smirk, "Go make me a drink?" I'd go running into the kitchen, excited to have a task, to be able to help out where I could, with no awareness that what he asked of me was wrong. I'd grab his glass and add ice. Then measure out the vodka carefully, knowing he preferred it on the heavier side, pour in some grapefruit juice and gently mix it up. I carefully walked it back to him hoping it would be satisfactory. If I was good, he would let me have a sip. I was so proud to make those drinks. There he'd sit for the rest of the evening, drinking his vodka and grapefruit juice, looking as if he was deep in thought, until it was time to make another. Eventually, he'd migrate to the bedroom—at which point he'd be blasted—cocktail in one hand, cigarette in the other.

While upstairs, he'd lay in the bed, doze off and the lit cigarette would fall from his hand and land on the carpet. The life saving wool blend of the gold colored carpet was so cheap it would put out the cigarette, avoiding a major house fire, time and time again. On his side of the bed there were at least 25 to 30 burn marks. When my mom finally replaced their bedroom carpet, she kept little pieces of leftover carpet under the bed that she would change out after he left more marks. In the simplest of terms, JB was a broken man. When he wasn't busy nearly burning down the house or ordering cocktails from the seven-year-old bartender, I don't know what he did, but he sure as shit wasn't busy teaching me how to maneuver in this world or teaching me about integrity, about ambition, pride, honor, or respect. In short, he never taught me how to be a man or prepare me for life in any kind of way. Shame on him for leaving me to fend for myself in this world but part of me is very thankful I didn't pick up any of his bad habits so I guess that's a blessing in disguise.

Every now and then he'd smile and laugh and we would all be at ease for a little while.

Back then, my young, undeveloped mind only saw what was in

front of me. There I was, a little boy with a mind ready to be taught and molded, but no dependable father to do it.

This left me impressionable, and had it not been for others in my life, I could have been lost like so many other kids in our world. So many young black kids—uncared for, neglected, left to raise themselves and learn how to become a man on their own.

And so, whether intentional or not, I sought out such lessons from other people knowing I could never rely on my own damn father.

When I was four, two years after I tripped and hit my head on my Mom Mom's coffee table leaving that nasty scar, my older cousin Nimmy came to pick me up at my parents' place. We were supposed to head down to Pop Pop's restaurant, which was around the corner from my parents' two-bedroom apartment.

He was born James Tuggle, but we all just called him Nimmy. Tall, muscular and lean, charismatic, smart and 5 or 6 years older than me. He gave off a "don't fuck with me" presence.

Nimmy and I had stopped at a gas station that his father worked at and then we crossed the street. Just then, Nimmy saw this little boy, who was about my age, playing in the dirt in front of his house. For a reason I couldn't understand, Nimmy gave me a tug and said, " You see that boy right there? If you don't go fuck him up, I'm gonna fuck you up."

I was only four years old when I had to learn how to fight in the streets.

Nimmy was more like an older brother to me. You see, he came from a broken home and his relationship with his father wasn't great either, so he was able to look out for me and provide guidance unlike anyone else. I respected him. I looked up to him. I loved him and he was family. That meant something to me. Always has, even then. So, when he told me to kick that kid's ass, I listened—because I trusted him.

The little boy's older brother came out of the house as I was walking towards him.

You see, Nimmy used to fight with the older brother. They already had beef. The brother must have seen the look in my eye and Nimmy standing at a distance behind me. He picked up a shard from a glass bottle and threw it at me, nearly twenty yards away, and it hit me in my forehead, right in between my eyes. What happened next, it's hard to imagine. I wouldn't necessarily say I panicked, but I certainly wasn't calm. I turned around and went back toward Nimmy, falling down and he picked me up. I remember running down the street, holding Nimmy's hand because all I saw was red—literally—everywhere. Red cars. Red Nimmy. Red buildings. Red earth. Red everything. Blood was gushing down my face, in my eyes, in my mouth and all over the front of my clothes. Nimmy had to lead me to the restaurant while we ran as fast as lighting, and the next thing I knew, I was in the hospital getting the glass taken out of my forehead and the stitches put in, right next to my other scar. Thankfully, I didn't bleed to death.

Four years old and I was being taught how to fight. But Nimmy was only trying to get me ready for the mean streets of Norristown and man, would I need it.

As I got older, I used to fight all over Norristown—kids from the east end, the west end, the valley. I was in a lot of fights, and pretty much won all of them. Let's be clear, though: I never started any fights in my life, but I sure did whoop a lot of ass of the people who started shit with me.

It wasn't just fighting that Nimmy taught me. He also taught me how to talk to girls, how to dance, how to shake and bake while playing football and to be fearless on the basketball court. I love him and I'm proud to be his little cousin. I looked up to him and I respected him more than anyone else.

Meanwhile, JB was a father to his liquor. Nimmy, though, he was there for me and I know there will be people out there who may say shame on Nimmy, that it was Nimmy's fault I got hurt, that Nimmy put me in harm's way. Well then, those people clearly aren't from Norristown. You see, in Norristown, you aren't given respect at random. You gotta *earn* respect and you don't back down. And you don't just suddenly become tough. You have to learn how to *be* tough.

Nimmy loved me and understood this. Because it was our way of life. It was how we had to be in order to survive where we lived. I think Nimmy knew that I didn't have a strong father figure. Nimmy was in my house and saw those burn marks on the carpet. He smelled the liquor on JB's breath. He saw the way JB staggered when he walked and how JB would stare at me as if I wasn't his real son. So Nimmy stepped up and stepped in where he knew no one else would. Nimmy wanted me to succeed; Nimmy wanted me to be resilient. And that's a whole lot more than either of my dads ever did for me.

JB's refusal to hold down a job took a toll on our family. A lot of the poor families in Norristown at that time used kerosene as an alternative heat source. So, when our main heater broke one day, my mother didn't replace it because she wanted to see how long it would take for JB to man up and fix it himself. Taking care of his family was clearly secondary to the alcohol.

He never bothered to get the heater fixed.

Instead, we were forced to use those cheap kerosene heaters to keep our entire house warm. You remember the ones—the little R2D2 looking things. Rectangular, yet round. Tan with slits all around it. JB had brought them home from his delivery driving job at Zummo's Hardware Store. I don't know how our house never burnt down.

At nighttime, because we didn't have any hot water, I had to boil huge pots of water and carry them upstairs to pour into the tub so our family could bathe every night.

JB always went first.

Then my mom.

Then me.

And then my little sister.

In the dirtiest of water.

And when I'd step out and dry off, the house would be so cold that I'd immediately put on the clothes I was going to wear to school the next day, and they reeked of kerosene.

There I'd be, showing up to Middle School smelling like a gas station, like I hadn't bathed in weeks. And no matter how well

Nimmy taught me to fight, I still got teased. And since I couldn't fight everyone, I had to learn restraint, but I was very sad and embarrassed.

Here's something you gotta understand about growing up poor: when you're young, you don't realize what poor is, especially if you're born into it. Standing in government food lines was normal for us. Block cheese and dehydrated milk went a long way and just as I had no clue JB was my stepfather, I had no clue we were the have nots. But little by little, as you get older and the different levels of poor start to reveal themselves—or, rather, the different levels of well-off start to reflect on you from the outside world—it creates some real feelings of sadness and confusion about the haves and the have nots. And getting teased because of those horrible kerosene fumes made me realize that I no longer wanted to be a have-not.

I fucking hated being poor.

I was still in Middle School, JB was acting like a stranger as usual, my Uncle Dave came in and filled some holes like Nimmy did.

In the summertime while growing up, my mom used to take me up to my grandma's house to play with the other neighborhood kids while she worked. Me and my boys, Rodney, Louis aka "Big Stuff" and Adie Simmons, Terry and Anton Savage, James Boone, Stacy and Bernard Clark, Binky Johnson, Terry Dudley, my amazing cousins Lenton, Sean and Izek Tuggle would run around playing all day, riding bikes, playing sports, building forts and getting dirty, and when my mom would come to get me around five, I'd be filthy and tired. Uncle Dave must have noticed because one day he pulled me aside and said, "Listen, those other little kids, they live here. They can go home and get changed into clean clothes. You can't. You don't live here. You just come for the day and then you go home. You need to be clean when your mom comes to get you."

I didn't understand why it mattered back then, but I listened— because I trusted him. You see, there's a difference between having a father figure and having a deadbeat for a father figure.

And when a real man steps up in your life, whether conscious or not, you acknowledge it and trust it. Because what else can you possibly do? Uncle Dave Tuggle very likely saw my situation, knew about JB, and decided enough was enough with the perpetuating stereotype of deadbeat black fathers. So much so, that when all the other kids in the neighborhood had bikes and my family couldn't afford one, Uncle Dave did me a solid; he walked around the neighborhood, into back alleys and trash cans, collecting all sorts of bike parts so he could put a bike together for me. I will always love him for that. Of course I was the man when it came to riding BMX bikes too. I was the first one to bunny-hop over a tennis court net which had the whole town talking.

West Washington Street was the hub of the community. JB's mom and my mom's parents lived on that same street. It was lively and there was always something going on—family members popping in and out, someone cooking steak and peppers, fried chicken, or even a whole pig. When I was three, my mom and JB moved into their own two-bedroom apartment to save money. When I was five, we moved to 47 W. Basin Street where they bought a house and we had to feel out a new community. We still went over to Mom Mom and Pop Pop's since they only lived ten-minutes away, but it was still isolating for me, and I couldn't really make sense of it at first, so I started to lead two different lives and as I got older and started making a name for myself, it became easier to blend them into one.

When I was four, and we lived in that two-bedroom apartment, my sister was born. And she didn't look anything like me. Her features were different, her skin much lighter. And as a kid, you don't really understand consciously why you feel weird about it, but the feeling is still there. And it really messed with me. Especially at such an early age where everything you learn, feel and experience gets embedded into your psyche.

Where family life swelled with disappointment except for the occasional Uncle Dave and Nimmy rescue, school sucked just about as bad. In elementary school, I remember these two larger kids who were bullies—Jarrod Roseboro and Emmitt Culbreath, used to slam my head against the classroom door. It was painted blue and was made of steel with a little glass window in it and nearly every day, Jarrod and Emmitt would be there ready to show me and my best friend Jason Duff the what's what.

I remember feeling so scared and helpless. It was embarrassing and humiliating to have that done to me in front of all the other kids. I thought of Nimmy and all his wisdom. My back was against the wall, and I knew that I had to face this head on and I could not back down.

Before Jason and I walked the half mile to elementary school one day, I went into JB's bedroom and found his pocketknife—one of many possessions that had his initials on it. I slipped it into my pocket because I was determined to fight back once and for all. Emmitt and Jarrod were getting stabbed just like I saw people do on TV.

During the day, I headed back to class from a bathroom break and pulled out the knife to check and make sure the blade would come out quickly. Because that was how I imagined it going down. Quick and easy, just like how they handled my daily head bashings.

Just as I flipped it open, I heard "Hey Lenny, let's see what you have there." It was my music teacher.

I was immediately taken to the Principal's office.

I'll never forget him asking why I brought the knife to school in the first place. My answer to Mr. Bender?

"Show and tell."

Growing up, I didn't always feel safe in my environment. I couldn't find the courage to tell him that I was being severely bullied every day. I was frozen by fear. You see, that's the kicker when you lack a strong educated parental figure in your life: you're not always taught how to communicate or ask for help so instead, it usually manifests as a cry for help. If you're lucky, an adult will catch wind of what's going on or figure it out in time and provide resources to help. If it's not spotted in time, it could possibly turn into something more dangerous where other people can get hurt, kind of like what we see on the news. Diversity and Inclusion is not just for people of color. Everyone in this country would benefit if people were nicer to each other and learned about the things that make us all special.

JB came to the school in his work truck—ZUMMO HARD-WARE plastered right on the side—and he took me home to beat the shit out of me. Not once did he ask me why I would take his knife to school. I'm sure he just thought that it was his and I didn't have a right to touch his shit. There was absolutely no emotional intelligence in him and when he was done, there was no chatter, he silently drove me right back to school, where Jarrod and Emmitt were waiting. Nothing changed and I was bullied again.

All I remember after my ass whoopin was how much shame I felt, how much anger. But in retrospect, I just wished I'd had the courage to tell someone what was happening to me. I wished I had a father who I could trust and who could advocate for me and my friend Jason because he didn't have a dad in his life. One day though, we had enough and started fighting back. We caught Emmitt by himself and beat his ass. Another time, we saw Jarrod walking alone and started pelting him in his head with rocks. They left us alone after that and Jason is still one of my best friends to this day. Funny thing is that I spoke on the phone with Jarrod in 2021. He said he heard that Emmitt had died. I made him apologize to me and then we called Jason and he apologized to him as well. On July 4th 2023, Jarrod and I had lunch together at my upscale private social club in Los Angeles. He thanked me for not stabbing him or telling my mother because my mom and his mom were friends. His mother was a sweetheart but I'm sure she would have beat his ass if she knew about it.

As a little sponge, I really didn't understand it then but, watching my grandfather start that restaurant was the first time I ever saw someone start their own business. And to have someone who looked like me start a business—even better.

Unfortunately, I never got to see him succeed financially because, as I understand it, anytime the restaurant would make a profit, my uncles would swoop in and steal the prize. And to this day I wonder what their life would have been like if they hadn't reaped what wasn't theirs, had the restaurant been able to thrive as it should have. You see his Soul Food restaurant could have provided so many opportunities for my family, so much money. Hell, I would bet that I wouldn't have been the first millionaire in my family.

Either way, I started to catch on. Little sparks of inspiration were forming inside me, whether conscious or not. Those sparks —the bullying at school, which most often stemmed from issues related to us being poor, and watching my Pop Pop run his restaurant—were igniting a fire of inspiration that changed my 8 year old mentality from, "I hate being poor" to "I hate being poor, so what do I do about it?"

As I got older, I'd walk through the neighborhood and look for opportunities. My favorite was stopping by JB's mom's house. Now remember, I didn't know Gertrude wasn't my biological grandmother until the end of eighth grade. I just thought of her as grandma. And my God, she loved me just as any biological grandmother would love her real grandson. Never did I have a reason to think she wasn't my blood.

When I'd walk by her house, I'd always ask her if she needed anything—not because I wanted to make a buck, but because I loved her and wanted to make sure she was taken care of. See, that's key to being an entrepreneur, I'd later find out—if you lead with love (as compared to a cheap obsession with making money), you'll find success faster. So, I'd ask her if she needed anything and almost always, she needed her lawn mowed, so I'd pull out her rusty old lawn mower and go up and down, up and down until the job was done, expecting nothing in return. But every single time, she'd give me ten dollars, a kiss on the forehead, and a handful of grapes off her grapevines in the backyard. The grapes were a little too sour for me, but I never told her that. I'm sure my face did, though.

Usually after I finished my rounds and earned a little cash here and there, I'd head home and watch TV in my parents' bedroom. There were a few different shows I'd watch, but the show that always reeled me in was *Dynasty*, you know, the show about the rich white family the Carringtons.

It was about a wealthy family in the oil industry. They gathered for cocktail hours in their living room in fancy gowns and tuxedos, drove luxury cars, and had sprawling mansions and owned horses.

You know, rich people shit. It's what gave me the definition and understanding of what a millionaire looked like. Up until then, I had no clue that real people lived like that. I'll never forget one time I watched it and saw Blake Carrington and his conniving ex-wife Alexis, played by John Forsythe and Joan Collins respectively, bitching about one thing or another in the Carrington mansion. I thought, Hold up, y'all have all this time and money to just… cause drama?

At first, I couldn't believe it, but by the end of the episode, my attitude shifted. It wasn't "Y'all are just too damn dramatic," but rather, it became, "I. Want. *That*." Not the drama or the ex-wives or even the money, in a sense; I wanted the freedom that the money allowed. You see, at that time I believed that millionaires didn't have to worry about their father being such a disgraceful drunk that he'd get fired from every job, leaving the family with no money for food, electricity or heat in the crib. Millionaires didn't have to worry about getting bullied or worry about how they will pay for college. Millionaires didn't have to learn how to fight at four years old. And let's face it: millionaires didn't have to take baths in filthy water that the rest of the family had already used.

I. Wanted. That.

And so, I studied them. I watched the way they walked, the way they talked, the way they handled delicate situations. Everything they did, I wanted to do the same. Back then, there's no way I thought about it like this, but in retrospect, I was learning how to manifest. I was learning how to take baby steps toward larger goals. Back then, I thought of it this way: when I become a millionaire, I'm gonna need to know how to behave like one, so I better start learning now.

And then: Nick Kimball. Y'all remember him? He was the hard-working, successful drill foreman played by the gifted actor, director, and philanthropist Richard Lawson. I was just sitting there in front of the TV, daydreaming as I studied these rich white people when BAM—here comes this elegant black man who looked like me. On a show of about ninety-nine percent of white people doing rich white people shit, he was charming and debonair, well-spoken with impeccable style. At first, this hit me as kind of funny. I sat there in JB's three-bedroom house, the burn holes in the carpet, the scent of kerosene stained into the furniture and walls, and a father figure who didn't mean shit to me. And there on the TV was a fresh-looking black man who carried himself well, like a real man should, and had everything I wanted. Nick Kimball. Why couldn't someone like that be my father?

In one of my favorite episodes, Nick invites the stunning Dominique Deveraux, played by the incomparable Diahann Carroll, to dinner, whisking her away on a private jet to San Francisco. He had class and all the right moves. In flight, they eat caviar and drink champagne. And then it hit me: I don't need a good dad to be successful, or to fly in a private jet that has champagne and caviar. You see, it wasn't anger, spite or resentment—although I sure felt those toward JB on the regular. Rather, it was a yearning and a deeper understanding on another level that one day I, too, would be a millionaire, just like Nick Kimball. I just didn't know how or when. But I knew, I sure as hell was going to be rich and that I would be getting out of Norristown.

FIVE

Winning and Losing

There was this industrial laundromat across from my grandparents' home on Washington Street. It was a large brick building and, when I was little, my friends and I would look through the large windows and watch the women—and some men—doing laundry. Every day, no matter the circumstances, employees were there scrubbing, brushing, drying and pressing. Hard workers, they were. Which was very confusing to me. We were always told that if you work hard and do your best, you could make something of yourself in this world, that you'd be able to have a good life. And everywhere I looked were hard workers— my mom, my grandparents, most of my family, most everyone in my neighborhood, the folks in the laundromat. So why then, if they were busting their asses, were they living paycheck to paycheck and not millionaires like the people on *Dynasty*?

All around us there was some kind of money-making going on: my grandfather with his restaurant (well, for as long as that lasted), crooked street hustlers, drug dealers, pimps and sex workers, my mom worked part-time as a bartender at the Gold Star, other parents were out there taking odd jobs and there were a few people walking the streets recycling cans and bottles. A whole lotta money making, but not a whole lotta thriving. And I quickly learned the right ways to earn a buck and the wrong ways. You see, at the end of the day after the final bell rang in middle school, us kids would go over to Mr. Dewdrops, this store on the corner of Freedley and Powell Streets, where we'd play video games and hang out. And right next to the door was a big tub of candy. Like Jolly Ranchers or some shit. So, one day, I grabbed the entire bucket and ran out.

The next day in school, I sold the candy to the kids from the suburbs who had some extra money. I was running penny candy for ten cents a pop. Oh, I thought I was making money! I couldn't believe how easy it was. And I couldn't understand why JB didn't have my new entrepreneurial sense. I thought he was a fool. It's this easy to make money and there he is squandering his days away at the hardware store or whatever job he was clinging to that month. Why couldn't he just sell shit on the side and up the price?

And just like that, as quick as the gig started, it came to an end. The next day at school there was an announcement.

"If anyone knows who stole the candy from Mr. Dewdrops store, please report them to the office."

I was so frightened. But you know what? No one snitched on me. Sixth, seventh and eighth graders, and not one person ran their mouths and told on me. Can you believe that? Talk about the spirit of Norristown.

Mr. Dewdrop, I doubt you're still alive, but if you are, that was my bad and I apologize.

That fear, though, stuck with me and that was the wrong way to earn a buck. And if it made me that scared, I wasn't about to pursue it. Who wants to go through life like that?

I knew there had to be a better way to make some money. I learned a valuable lesson.

When we weren't scheming up new ways to make a few bucks like carrying old ladies' groceries to their car for change or mowing lawns or selling lemonade from our stand on the street, we were break-dancing and pop-locking in the library parking lot or at Darrell Moses Crib. On any given day, most of us neighborhood kids could be found playing one sport or another or chasing girls on the block.

The crew always rallied by word of mouth. "Yo, Carlos Brown and Mark Zaczkiewicz! Go get Curt Henning, Mikey Rogus, Shawn McGuffey and Dante Lewis. Yo, Rich Williams, Barry and Jeff Pierce, go get Rob Horton, Kem Johnson, Johnny Carbone, Shaun Chatman and the others. Gonna play ball down at the library, three o'clock." And just like that, we balled out.

We were always outside playing—wiffle ball, kickball, street hockey, basketball, football, hide and go seek, riding bikes, running through the opened water fire hydrant, you name it. It must have been somewhere between the age of 6 or 8 when I became conscious of something special percolating inside of me— not just a skill, but a raw talent. When we would ride bikes, when we'd play tag, and even sports like baseball and football, I started to stand out. Now, I would eventually grow up to be the man, but I was a little guy back then. Two things though, I was fast and coordinated. If I had to guess, my suspicion would be that it was ancestral.

You see, Mrs. Gwen Bazemore, aside from being a Bell Telephone extraordinaire, was also a superstar athlete. For years she played volleyball and was, like mother like son, the coveted team member, always picked first, always fought over, and a leader, eventually becoming captain of the team. As if that wasn't badass enough, she played softball too, forming an all-black women's team called the Thunderbolts that won the women's slow-pitch championship a few years in a row.

And Hampton, was a track star at Norristown High.

As for JB, he did nothing but that doesn't matter because he was not my real dad anyway.

The first time I was part of organized sports was in the

Greater Norristown Football League when I was around 8 years old . I don't know how it works these days, but back then, all the kids were drafted to a team in the league. I was chosen to play for the Cardinals, and some of my friends got drafted to the Raiders.

Despite knowing I had a special talent inside me, I soon learned that natural talent wasn't enough. You also need intelligence to play sports. I'll never forget the first day of practice sitting there on the field, absolutely petrified as the coach explained how the game worked. I mean, I was so fucking scared because I had no clue what I was getting myself into. This guy was talking about cones here, holes there, offensive this and defensive line that, blocking formations and whatnot. And I was lost. We had played games all over our neighborhood; I was skilled, and I knew it. But this? How was I gonna keep up?

For 4 years straight, I played Pop Warner little league football for the Cardinals and for the first two years we came in last place. In my third year I got a whole lot better and we won our first championship. We were undefeated and unscored upon. We won the championship again in my 4th year and we shut out every team except the 1 touchdown the Raiders scored against us. We were so good that year that the league put together an Allstar team composed of the best players in the league and my Cardinals beat them too in the last game of that season.

Baseball was my second pastime and another sport I excelled in. Some would say I was better in baseball than I was in football. Now, this isn't me being cocky. This is me being real. There must have been something in the water over there in Pennsylvania because I felt like a young Jim Thorpe in a couple of ways. I was talented in every sport but unfortunately, my family didn't have the financial means to support me in the way that I needed. So, I went without baseball cleats or a glove, which are necessary to play baseball. The valuable lesson I learned in life is that, "It's not about what you don't have. It's all about doing what you can with what you do have!"

It was in the early 1980's and everyone wanted those shell top Adidas, you know, the ones with three stripes on them. Madonna,

Michael Jackson, Run DMC. Parachute pants, New Yorker shoe-strings and acid-wash denim were all in style. I remember I wanted those shell-tops sneaks so bad so I could be cool like the other kids who had them, but you know, we were poor and couldn't afford things like that. My mom owed me $15 for some gardening I had done for her, but instead of giving me the money, she bought me these orange sneakers with four black stripes. I was devastated.

"They look just like Adidas," she said, so convinced that there was no difference.

"No Mom, they don't," I said. "They got four stripes."

But I wore them anyway, and I loved her for trying, no matter how disappointed I was. She could have let me go without new shoes, but she tried her best. So, I wore them to school, thinking I could be slick and slide by. I was rocking those bright orange kicks with pride. I was fresh with a new style because everybody's sneakers were the same with 3 stripes and I convinced myself that mine were special because they had 4 stripes.

And then I heard someone say, "Lenny got Fadidas on! Fadi-das! (Fake Adidas) He got on Halloween kicks. Yo, man, why you got an extra stripe?"

I was mortified.

My best friend Jason Duff saw how embarrassed I was and how much my feelings were hurt, so after school, he took me up the street to this thrift shop called Fudgie Budgie where they had a pair of used Nikes.

"All you gotta do," he said, "throw these out the window and they're yours."

That was it—the solution to the fake Adidas.

And so, when no one was looking, I opened up the thrift shop window, I threw the Nikes right out, and shut it. Later that night, I went back and climbed over the fence and picked up my new used Nike sneakers.

Also, since I didn't have baseball cleats, it was those Nikes I wore. Mind you, they were way too big for my feet, and they were filthy like someone had rolled them around in the dirt. But, I was so damn proud and thankful to have a pair of name-brand shoes to wear to school and play sports.

There was this nice older gentleman, Mr. Scag Cottman, who was always around town. And anybody who wanted to play sports or who showed promise athletically, Mr. Cottman would try to help them, whether it was by finding a way into organized sports or donating his time where he could. He must have seen me exhibit a lot of promise because he gave me a pair of baseball cleats and Mr Cianciulli who lived on W. Fornance Street, gave me my first glove when I played for the Astros in the NAA Baseball Little League. (I remember we called him Mr. Chin-Chilly because it was easier.)

You see, God has this way of sending hope in your direction and filling in the empty holes in your life from time to time. Although Mr.Cianciulli and Mr Scag didn't fill in as a father figure, they sure helped me to be the best player I could be and I will alway love them for that. And I sure as shit was one of the best all around athletes to ever be born in Norristown, Pa.

I stole bases left and right and was never thrown out. I played little league when I was 7 or 8 and when we were 15 through 18, we would get invited to play ball against the inmates up at Graterford Prison. Behind those huge fences, I hit off and stole bases against grown men. Me, John Kitt, Mikey Rogus and the rest of the team would give them our sweatbands and batting gloves after the game. It was like Christmas morning for them. They showed so much joy in playing against us and the gifts we gave them afterwards. I felt joy as well by putting a smile on their faces. But it was those sneakers, cleats and glove that started it all.

In eighth grade, my fifth year of organized football, Mr. Scag organized a neighborhood tryout for the St. Patrick's football team but only a measly seven players showed up and none of us were Catholic. That ain't enough to have a real team, so he struck a deal with Holy Savior, which was a few blocks up the street from us. As part of the deal, we had to attend church and take a religious catechism class once a week called "CCD." They supplied us with uniforms and our teams effectively merged. They really didn't need us so I was thankful they let us play but little did they know they were getting me—a blossoming fucking baller in every sense of the word.

I'm sure there were a handful of reasons why I went from being a shy little kid to literally being the star of the show, but one major factor, I think, was watching the Raiders on Sunday and Monday Night Football. Man, their uniforms were so sick—that sleek black and silver—and I was jealous of my friends who were drafted to the Raiders in little league. The plays those NFL Raiders would make on Sunday and Mondays were insane. Moves that we would imitate when playing pick up games around the hood. Marcus Allen was amazing and one of my favorites to watch. The Raiders were the bad boys of the NFL at that time and I knew I wanted to play for them one day.

I think it was more than impressive moves though. By watching them, I learned team effort, unity, working toward a common goal and how to be a leader.

In the early 80's, there was this Pepsi and NFL bottle cap contest on TV that my cousin Lenton Tuggle Jr. and I would always see. Hidden under each Pepsi bottle cap was one of the twenty-eight NFL team helmets. Collect all twenty-eight and win something like $1000 bucks which was basically a million dollars to us kids in the hood.

But you know, our parents didn't have money to buy much of anything, let alone Pepsi after Pepsi because of some marketing campaign.

Right across the street from my middle school, was the Norristown Elmwood Park Zoo. And at the café, you had to step up onto this little wooden platform to be at the cashier's level. One day I noticed there were a bunch of coins between the slits of the platform laying on the ground. People must have dropped their change and it had to be over a long period of time because there were lots of coins trapped under there. So what did this kid from Norristown do? I bought a piece of gum, chewed it until it was all soft and sticky, I dried it off a little then put the gum on the end of a straw, and sat there for as long as I needed, getting all the coins out so I could buy more Pepsi.

And my God, were we close to winning the contest. Lenton and I only needed a few more teams but towards the end, everytime we bought a new Pepsi, it seemed that the Raiders would be under the caps—perhaps planting a subconscious seed guiding my lifelong fan loyalty to the team.

Although I never found them all, the endeavor still helped to solidify my tenacious attitude, which is foundational to my success. You see, I learned at a young age that you always have to continue asking yourself, "Now what?" Whether you're stuck and can't find a way forward or you may be riding the highs of success, if you learn to be an explorer of your future and ask yourself where can you go from here, you'll never be stuck for too long.

Seventh grade, 1983. The confidence seeped in. The fear went away, allowing my natural talents and ability to just do what they did best. My football team was growing stronger. We had a winner's mentality, all set to the beat of a Queen song. (We will, we will, rock you!)

I was a kicker, a nose guard, receiver and a running back. I remember one time playing wide receiver against the Jets and our quarterback David Mark threw the ball, I closed my eyes and kept running. I put my hands out and to my surprise, I caught the ball. I remember another time I was playing as a defensive back in a 9th grade high school game against Abington High. I was going back to cover the wide receiver and his quarterback overthrew us. I noticed the receiver gave up so I kept running as fast as I could. I jumped up, put my hand on the ball, lost my balance but as I was coming down trying to catch my balance, I saw the ball falling right in front of me—in slow motion—and before it hit the ground, I managed to kick the ball back up into the air, catching it and I ran it back for a touchdown.

I was a badass! It was the confidence and this newfound comfort in leadership ability that helped me take my team to success.

Now, when we'd play sports around the neighborhood,

everyone was picking me first. Every kids' dream, right? I won't lie, it was the fucking best. To be the kid everyone wants on their team—I took pride in that. I didn't have much, but I had my skill, and I started to believe that it would get me out of Norristown.

When the other teams would lose, they'd get mad. So naturally, they'd try to get me next time, and the pattern would repeat. Over time, I think some of those kids started to envy my abilities. But we were kids, you know? No one was really verbalizing it because emotionally we didn't know how to. As I got older and competition grew, I learned how to identify when it was happening because it started to manifest off the field too, you know, when it comes to girls or other shit that really shouldn't be important at that age. I could sense a little jealousy. What's worse is I was the one trying to get along with everybody. No drama, no bullshit. I wanted loyal friends, not enemies because when I didn't get the attention of my father, I looked for camaraderie in my peers and most of us came from broken homes so I thought they might be looking for the same.

There I was, a star athlete, and my own father hardly attended any of my games. Mom was there every time though. She was the biggest cheerleader in my life. Like I said at the beginning of this book, the women in my life did right by me. My dad fumbled the ball and made my home life a damn mess. For a kid, that's a really tough dichotomy to wrap one's head around. Wake up in the morning in an unwelcome home. Go to school and suddenly you're in an alternate universe. You're the cool kid, the one others look up to. After school, you hit the field and yet again, people praise the ground you walk on for being one hell of an athlete and person. In high school, when the game was over and I was done signing autographs, I headed home to where life wasn't easy anymore, where my father didn't seem proud of me, let alone care for me. That's a lot for a kid to process—if he can process it at all. And if he can't it builds up and eventually, something's got to give. Like a little hole in a dam. Eventually, it becomes a bigger problem if it's not addressed.

The Catholic league championship game of my eighth grade

year was a big deal. All championships are a big deal, but this one would have a major impact on me that would last my entire life. It was Holy Saviors vs. Visitation and my good friend Dave Raimondo was playing for the Visitation squad and was talking shit in school all week. I was determined to make a fuckin' mark in that game, held on Bishop Kenrick High School's football field, I scored three touchdowns, and I threw for a touchdown too. Our quarterback, Jacki Bruni pitched me the rock for a halfback option pass. I was running to the right, ball in hand and then stopped, planted my feet, and threw it to Jamal Adams as he was running down the left sideline. He jumped up, touched the ball, bobbled it, caught it and sped in for a touchdown to win the game.

Man, I've never heard an audience cheer like that before. The sidelines were packed and roared, so when Jamal scored, I knew it was over. Adrenaline was pulsing through every inch of my body as our team was celebrating and the crowd started closing in. Not only was I proud of myself, but I felt like I was making my family proud too. I saw my mom jumping up and down clapping and cheering. I wanted to cry tears of joy. This was it. Top of the world.

Here comes Mama Bazemore onto the field, so proud of me. She gave me a hug and told me the Director of Admissions for Bishop Kenrick Catholic High School wanted to meet me. So, we went over and exchanged courtesies. He congratulated me in a way that made me feel that I was important. That I had substantial value.

"Listen," he said, "I am aware of your family's financial situation, but we would love for you to attend Bishop Kenrick to play football for us."

Mom must have already known because she looked elated. I was shocked, and I'm sure my mouth was hanging open.

"You won't pay a dime," he said. "We will have a car pick you up at your house every day, so you can get to school. We'll supply you with school uniforms, books and a lunch card. You won't have to spend any money whatsoever. Just please come play football for us."

You see, he was offering me a full scholarship. A chance at a better future. A future that people like me, like the Tuggle's and Bazemore's, like most black folk who lived in Norristown couldn't afford. All I thought was, damn, that's really nice of him, but what about my friends who were all going to play football at Norristown High and not Bishop Kenrick?

"Thank you," I told him. "I'll have to think about it."

The man was kind. He told me it was fine if I took some time to think about it but let him know because they'd be honored to have me. I just couldn't shake the thought of being without my friends at Norristown High. These were the kids I grew up with. They were my people, my community, my family. We all had the dream of going to the High and playing football together. I didn't want to alienate them because I played with these kids every day in the hood. It would be so fucked up if I went to another school so I didn't go. You just don't do that to your family. Loyalty is one of those qualities that folks in Norristown valued so highly. That's what made us strong. That's what made us all resilient but at the same time, that opportunity might have been great for me.

SIX

Extreme Highs and Lows

"I wanna introduce you to someone else," my mom said right after the championship game. So, she took me over to the sidelines to this man and his family.

"Lenny," she said, "This is your real dad!" An extreme high to an extreme low!

"What?" I asked, completely blindsided.

"This is Hampton Coleman II, your biological father."

This, of course, meant that JB was not my biological father. And what's messed up is she didn't explain the discrepancy or why he was absent from my entire life. But somehow, she didn't have to. At that moment, although my teenage brain struggled with it, the shit started to make sense. It felt weird as fuck and it made me sick to my stomach. It was now clear that JB wasn't my real dad because my sister looked way different than I did. She was very light skinned and looked white when she was a baby. The man barely spoke to me my entire childhood and was basically, nonexistent despite living in the same household.

"You know," my mom said, "your dad wants you to come down for the weekend to stay with him."

This wasn't a question to see if I was interested. It was more of a command. And what's worse is she called him "my dad." Man, that shit made me feel like throwing up. I was completely unsure of who I was because my parents had been lying to me all of my young life.

Hampton, a United States Air Force Vet and Postal worker, was about 5 feet 10 inches tall with size 15 sneakers. Although his eyes and voice seemed sincere, he was quiet, expressing little emotion—a trait that has affected me since I met him. So quiet that it made you wonder what could have happened to him in his life to make him so void of expressive affection. And so, the next weekend, Hampton came up to Norristown to pick me up and take me back to his place in Camden, NJ. He said that I could go hang out in his backyard but I couldn't go out front because a few people were recently killed on the street because of drug activity.

When he came to pick me up at my mom's house, I got in the back of the car and in the front seat was Hampton and his wife Mae. Secured in the back seat was a little baby, my new half-brother Hampton Coleman III. He and I would go on to have a great relationship over the years. I loved him dearly and It was hard to see him pass away from lymphoma cancer at only 25 years of age. He was nice, smart, good looking, funny and very protective of me. Love and miss you little bro! (b. February 25, 1984 - d. April 11, 2009.)

First stop on this bizarre fucking trip was to Syms clothing store in Cherry Hill, NJ so they could buy me some gear for school. The car ride was dead silence as we drove to new areas that I had never seen before. My life was completely turned upside down. I tried to pretend that it was a new adventure but my mind kept focusing on the fact that my life was now different. I was so unsure of my identity while riding in the back of that stranger's car. I was so scared and I thought my mind was playing tricks on me. I could not tell if everything that was happening to me was real. At the end of that weekend, he dropped me back off at my mom's house and there was a part of me that felt special because I knew who my real dad was. At the same damn time, I couldn't help but to feel sadness for some of my friends who still didn't know who their dads were.

Feeling the need to get some answers, I only broached the topic once with Hampton on that weekend and I never really went back down to visit again until I was older. That weekend I asked him, "Where has he been?" To which he replied, "You know, when I came out of the Air Force, your mom and JB told me not to come around anymore. So, I didn't come around."

Years later when I'd ask my mom about this, her story matched Hampton's story to a T. Which is even more disturbing because their response kept the entire topic surface level. There was no talk about how it affected me, how it affected them, how it severely hindered my ability to trust people or feel safe at a young age. Nothing. It was just two simple sentences. And then it was history. For them, that is.

I remember being expected by my mother to wear the new clothes Hampton bought me for school that next Monday. And I'll never forget how weird it was for me to wear those fucking clothes. At home, JB seemed even more distant now that I knew the truth. Do you know how hard it is for a young teen to process all of this?

Too fucking hard. Absolutely too fucking hard!

Around this time, us 13 year old neighborhood kids did what neighborhood kids do. We would occasionally sneak into our parents' alcohol cabinets and take what we could without getting noticed. This was still the beginning of hip hop and rap, so we were seeing these strong black men drinking forty-ounce beers and we wanted to be like them. I remember seeing this TV commercial with this cool ass brotha, Billy D. Williams advertising Colt 45. Talking about it works every time. I remember we used to sneak into my friends Wendy DeFazio and Jimmy Bailey's back shed. I don't think their dad ever missed the 12 oz beer cans of "Old Milwaukee" we took. (Their parents were some of the nicest people I ever knew.)

I remember one time after a football game, a few of my friends and I went up to Via Veneto's Pizza Shop and ate Sicilian thick crust pizza, which is much better than any Detroit or

Chicago style pizza. We were drinking Wild Irish Rose. You know, the alcohol you don't want to fuck with. We ended up getting so drunk and sick that we quickly realized we ain't touching that shit ever again. In the hood, sipping on Wild Irish Rose was like a rite of passage.

Eighth grade was the first time I got high. I was hanging with a close friend in my neighborhood named Shawn McGuffey (Rip), another kid who didn't know who his father was. His mom Patty was a classic hippie. She was awesome and had velvet posters and huge soft bean bags on the floor, multicolored area rugs all over. It was so chill hanging out in their apartment. Shawn took some of his mom's stash and we went down to Roosevelt Field to play some football. Before the game, we went under the bleachers and I asked him, what do we do with it? And so he taught me how to roll it up all neat and then he told me to smoke it. I'm like, you do what? How? So, he taught me how to light it, puff it and inhale it. And just like a first timer, you know how they do it, I started coughing up a lung, thinking I did it wrong. After a few hits, I said, "Man, this shit don't work." Next thing I knew, fifteen minutes went by and I was spaced out of my mind. This period was a true coming of age where we watched and learned from the older kids drinking and getting high in our neighborhood. We wanted to be cool like them and they would let us join in, cigarette smoking and all.

I had several groups of friends in different neighborhoods that I would play with. On one scorching hot summer day, I was hanging with the group of white boys that I met while in middle school and while participating in the Catholic sports program. We always kept it tight, and we kept it light. We rode BMX bikes a lot that summer. Me and some of my football championship winning teammates got along great. These kids were mostly Italian and Irish. There were usually around thirteen of us who would ride bikes all over. You know, actin' like we owned the streets. Not because we were arrogant kids, but because we were proud to be from Norristown.

One of the kids in the group was Rick Gallo. His family was

considered to be the biggest slumlords in the entire Norristown area. Rick's father was an Italian man who purchased a bunch of dilapidated properties. With little to no renovations, he would rent these places to the black folks of Norristown who couldn't afford anywhere else to live. He'd cash in check after check with hardly any upkeep or compassion for his tenants. And some would say that's how they became millionaires over time. But anyway, it was a hot summer night after the sun went down. We were getting tired of cruising the streets on our bikes when Rick shouted, "Hey everyone, let's go swimming at my house. Everybody except Jules because he's the youngest, and Lenny because he's black."

Rick looked me right in the eyes and then said, "My dad doesn't like black people." Just then Mike Ciriello, Jules' older brother looked at me with disbelief and empathy. He obviously didn't know what to say or do but since he and the other white kids were allowed to go, off they went. Mike is still one of my closest friends and when I spoke to him and Jules in 2022 about that night, we all agreed that it had a lifelong deep effect on the three of us. But mostly on me.

Before that moment, it never really occurred to me that I was all that different because of the color of my skin. And when he said that, it smacked me right across the fucking face. For the first time in my young life, I became conscious of the fact that skin color mattered to an *ignorant person*. It's only pigmentation, not some incurable contagious disease! Man, that was a painful and disgusting realization.

Jules and I decided to follow them and hide in the bushes next to the pool. We heard and watched them swimming and laughing and having a great time. And just then Jules stepped on a twig and it snapped—just like in the movies. Rick heard it and yelled, "Hey Jules! Is that you?" No response. "Jules! Is that you.?"

Jules finally answered "yeah."

"Shit, you can come! But Lenny can't."

Jules turned and looked at me, very sad before saying that he was sorry.

And he slowly walked out from behind the bushes and joined

them in the pool. I sat there crying as I watched those white boys swim in Rick's pool as if it was heavenly after a long hot day of riding bikes. I was a black kid not allowed in a pool simply because Rick Gallo's dad didn't like black people even though he made his money off of them.

I picked up my bike and walked down the dirt path that was near the football field where Rick and my other teammates helped me win the eighth-grade football championship just two weeks before. Rick and I remained casual friends after that because he was just a kid too and I didn't think it was his fault that his father was liked that. The Gallos' lived in one of the biggest houses in Norristown on DeKalb Street, with a nice driveway and mani-cured landscaping. When I crossed the street and turned around to look at his house, I said to myself, one day, I will be able to buy that fucking house. And I was going to be able to afford ten other houses if I wanted them. And I was going to live in a house on a hill overlooking the town. Just like rich people do.

I realized on that day, on that slow confusing journey home, that my blackness was not a weakness. It was my strength and that certain people may be scared of it. It was just something that was part of who I am and for better or worse, I was different and I was probably going to have to deal with something like that for the rest of my life!

By the time I started ninth grade at Norristown High School, after meeting my real father Hampton, my entire life had changed. Everything felt like a huge fucked up lie. And this new father figure who seemed to be a deadbeat just like my stepfather JB, coupled with being poor and experiencing racism firsthand, was taking its toll on me.

I started missing the school bus on purpose a couple of times a week so I could drink a forty-ounce of beer and smoke a joint on my walk to school. By the time I got to class, I had to have smelled like beer and weed. And not one person said a thing. Oftentimes when people drink and smoke to that extreme, it's a cry for help. For me, I was in a dark self destructive place and it was a cry for help to ease the pain until someone at school noticed. But, no one ever noticed!

At one point around this time, my mother put me in therapy. You see, mothers alway know when something's wrong and I guess she noticed that my behavior changed some.

I was reluctant to go to therapy. What was so wrong with me that I needed therapy? The thought of it scared me. So, I asked if I could bring 2 of my friends, Manny and Jerry, two kids from my neighborhood who lived on Spruce Street. They were poor, too. They understood what I was going through. They were my support system and I needed them to help me get through the fear. The therapist agreed and said they could come. But when we arrived, he said they had to wait outside in the hallway behind the closed door. How fucked up? I was so frightened. At that moment, the therapist broke my trust. All I knew was I wasn't as scared to go when Manny and Jerry were joining me, and now that they couldn't, that fear was back.

All I wanted to do was disappear. If I could just get out of that room and escape into a forty and a joint, everything would have been alright for a little while.

The therapist put me at a table in the middle of the room. On the table was a piece of paper and some number 2 pencils.

"What do you want to be when you grow up, Lenny?"

"An NFL football player," I said. Funny, in that small moment, I felt a little better—but only because I was thinking about the thing that made me special. That skillset I knew I possessed and the talent I thought would get me somewhere. The passion that would make my dreams of flying on a private jet eating caviar and drinking champagne come true.

"Why don't you draw me a picture of what you want to be when you grow up."

And so, I drew a football player. It took a few minutes.

"That's great," he said.

"Can I go to the bathroom?" I interrupted.

"Sure."

He opened the door, and I took off running. I left the office and ran all the way back home.

I never went back.

Which is such a damn shame. I obviously would have benefited from child therapy. What pissed me off the most is that my simple ask—to have Manny and Jerry join me in the room—would have benefited everyone. I would have felt more comfortable and opened up more. Manny and Jerry would have learned a thing or two since they were poor like me. And the therapist would have been able to work his magic on me. But instead, he broke my trust and I ran.

I wish this was not the case but, therapy and mental health treatment is not as prevalent in the black community as it needs to be. Call it what you want, blame it on what you want, but at the end of the day, we all know it's a systemic issue perpetuated by ignorance in our country.

The facts are clear. According to a study conducted by the Harvard School of Public Health, racial trauma is one of the reasons black people in some communities have higher rates of PTSD. A staggering 8.7 percent higher, when compared to white people. According to a study conducted by the University of Georgia, nearly 65 percent of black youth report traumatic experiences, compared to 30 percent of their peers from other ethnic groups. Furthermore, about 25 percent of blacks seek mental health treatment as compared to 40 percent of whites, according to McLean Hospital. Even worse, all of this has infiltrated our community, as one study by the National Alliance of Mental Illness shows 63 percent of black people believe that a mental health condition is a sign of weakness.

I could go on and on with statistics proving the ins and outs of the lack of mental health treatment for black people in America. But the fact of the matter is the numbers support the thesis: we need better access to mental health awareness, and we need to destigmatize those seeking help. Imagine what we could all contribute to society if we get the help we deserve?

Racism is a disease in this country and a huge part of the problem because it's destroying America. If you're reading this and you are white, most likely you may have a form of implicit bias so, I need you to check out these next few paragraphs very carefully if you want to understand where I'm coming from. And if you're black or a person of color, you're probably going to get it if you have an ounce of cultural competence and you are not in denial. It's unfortunate but race plays a role in our everyday life. These issues will not disappear on their own, so we should treat each other with a little more individual respect and kindness.

Educator Jane Elliott spoke to a room full of white folk that were seated, "I want every white person in this room who would be happy to be treated as this society in general treats our citizens, our black citizens, if you as a white person would be happy to receive the same treatment that our black citizens do in this society please stand." They all stayed seated. Nobody. Stood. Up! She went on to repeat it just in case they didn't understand the assignment. "If you white folks want to be treated the way blacks are in this society, stand!" Again, not one white person stood up. You see, you guys know what's going on in America and you see the way black people are being treated but you don't want it for yourselves or for anyone else in your family. It's so fucked up and disgusting that we as black people and our children have to continue dealing with this shit! Personally, I still get followed in stores by security on a regular basis and I could buy the whole damn building.

You see, I can change my financial status, but I can not change the color of my skin. The sad part is that, even if some of the security guards knew that I was wealthy, I'm convinced they would still follow me. I'm sure some white person knows this and makes off like a bandit because while security is eyeballing me, no one watches them. It's a sickness embedded in their mindset and other people in society have the same, watch out for the black person disease. We all know that this country needs more love, respect and equality for all, and it must start with the dismantling of systemic racism. Yes, It's a real thing that black people have to deal with every fucking day. Also, irresponsible political rhetoric and police brutality. No unarmed American or person should ever die in police custody. They should be able to stay alive and have their day in court. That's why I would recommend funding a program so that all police officers are given a psychological exam annually. They have a difficult job and should receive the support they deserve. Keeping society safe can be a traumatic everyday experience. Unfortunately, some police officers will take their work home with them, putting their own families at risk and domestic violence can be dangerous. We need to start helping them keep us safe in addition to keeping their families safe. We owe them that much!

Every one of us should have a fair shot at the American Dream however individuals come to define it for themselves. I'm simply talking about wholesome fairness in this melting pot country and a quality unbiased free education should be a right. Most black folk don't want or need a handout but they have been beaten down in every way by society so badly that they give up on the American Dream and then get called "Lazy." They just want a fair shot at building something for themselves and their families just like anyone else. The amount of stupid and unnecessary racial bull-shit that black people are forced to deal with from birth to death is so fucked up! You can help by just being nice when you see a person of color walking by and try giving them the benefit of the doubt or judge them by the way they treat you as an individual. Not just stereotype them because of some unfair and disproportionate media coverage on crime.

And since it's a two-way street, black folk should also realize that most white people are good people who are sympathetic to black injustice. They may not wish to trade places and deal with the lifelong struggle of racism that we face everyday and that is perfectly fine. However, some are part of our families and our work or friend groups. They are not out to harm our advancement in the world or destroy our invaluable black culture. We are strong people who have endured it all and will wake up tomorrow and do it all over again and again. America should be more gracious towards its black citizens. We helped build this entire country and we have almost 1.8 trillion dollars in buying power.

Also, while I'm at it, there is no such thing as black on black crime if there is no such thing as white on white crime. In my opinion, all of it should just be labeled crime! So, stop saying that dumb shit.

Hey now! Just to let you know, this isn't a feel sorry for me story. This is a story of fortitude and resilience while going through hardship and pain. Ultimately, surviving and thriving in life.

Although I was well known with a lot of friends, my high school years were tough. Depression really started to set in as I struggled to manage the massive issues that a child or young adult shouldn't have to deal with. You remember those don't you? Issues such as food insecurity, two deadbeat dads, bullying, racism and poverty. That was a heavy burden on my shoulders and my mind. And I dealt with it by drinking, doing drugs and partying. Being active in sports helped to take my mind off some of it but it did not solve everything. I was searching for anything I could find to distract me from my life. Because ultimately, I was angry that all of this was happening to me and I felt like I was all alone in the world. I didn't have educated adults in my life who could help me through my issues. It's not that the responsible adults in my life didn't care, or were poor role models. Rather, it was that no one had ever helped them and they didn't have the tools or education to communicate with me to make things better.

Education is so important in the world. It's another variable that can separate some people's income and quality of living. Like I said, the lack of resources in not just black communities, but impoverished communities' as well, hurts everyone because people can easily get left behind and disenfranchised from getting a piece of the American pie. I believe that having a good education and a willingness to continue learning can balance the playing field. Especially in the 6 main job sectors as technology and innovation make huge advances, (Healthcare, IT, Real Estate, Education, Retail and Government.) The gap between the haves and the have nots will keep getting wider causing more issues for all people of color, poor uneducated white people and immigrants too. Continuing education is vitally important. Honestly, I'm extremely proud of my mother. She is a great woman and did the best she could back then with the little she had and she is incredibly intelligent and resilient.

I knew that as a young black kid from a humble town, I didn't have a lot of options to get out. I had these big dreams of owning a house like Gallo's dad. I wanted so badly to make it out, not just for me, but for my family too. Because if I could get out, maybe I could help lift them up, as well.

Every year, Bishop Kenrick High School would host a carnival in the parking lot near their football field. While walking around and before my junior year in 1986, Howard Flowers told me that he wanted to introduce me to his friend Kathy Barnes- this pretty, smart and athletic Irish girl who was also funny and had a good sense of humor.

And you know, I tried to play it cool with a simple, "What's up?" And she hits me back with an equally chill, "Hey, what's up?"

She and I talked for a while and enjoyed the carnival. As we walked towards the front entrance, a car rolled by and some white dude yelled the N-word at me. So, I chased the car halfway down the block when, to my surprise, they got caught at the red light. I dove through the open passenger side window and fucked those two guys up. The driver put the car in park, and I beat both of their asses right in the front seat. My boys opened the door and pulled me out of the car. I brushed off and went right back to my conversation with Kathy. Like a real-life Shaft.

Kathy and I started dating soon after that night and for a while, things were cool.

Right before the football season started, Coach Grove asked me into his office and told me to switch up my playing style. Now understand that my style was unique to me, as it is for most athletes. It's what made me as good as I was. It's why I was revered by so many. It's why I was recruited by top universities across the country. And he wanted me to change that. I didn't understand this because I wasn't even the starting running back on varsity yet.

"I want you to run straight north and south, not zig-zag because that's what coaches are going to want from you when you get to college." He said.

Wow! What was I gonna do, say no? And so, I did exactly what he said even though it was a very old way of thinking. Now, I don't think he did this nefariously. I know in retrospect of course, he thought he was helping me by looking forward to my college career and I truly believed he cared for me deeply. The other part of me thinks he simply didn't understand how to cultivate and utilize my talent, ultimately containing me and not allowing me to grow my skills and abilities. In the first game of that season, I ended up returning a kickoff and when I ran to the left, I remember seeing Kevin Every blocking a defender but some other player slipped through and as I tried to cut it back to the right to avoid him, I stepped on his foot and twisted my ankle. The pain shot up my leg. My left ankle was broken and I sat out the entire season of my 11th grade year.

I played on the sophomore squad with my boys. I also played on the varsity team in 10th and 11th grade and not every under-classmen had that chance. The teams we played were all the same and we beat them year after year.

When me and my boys were seniors, we thought we would win every game but ended up going 9-3. Ever since I was little, I was always one of the best if not the best player on the entire field. I always played the entire game on both sides of the ball because of my athletic ability. In my senior year, I only had 12 interceptions and 12 touchdowns in 12 games and in the All-Star game that year, I scored 2 touchdowns and was MVP for the North team. Marshall Roberts from Abington was MVP for the South team. I admired him as a player and as a person. He went on to play at Rutgers University in New Jersey and I watched him play on TV. The most touchdowns I ever had in a single game was on my 8th grade team when I scored 7 and on my 9th grade team I scored 5 so, I always felt like I could have done more in my last year of high school if he didn't make me change my playing style.

What Coach Grove didn't understand is that most of us grew up together or played against one another in little league. We were all very coachable and knew how to play. We had an existing synergy that helped us build a winning bond on and off the field. Why change it? All he did was cause strife between me and my friends. They saw the change in my mood, but I didn't think I could tell them that the coach pulled me aside to change my playing style, completely unaware that a few of them had similar conversations with him. So, on the field, when that synergy was lost, we felt helpless. Mostly because we knew—as some of us ballers did—that our athleticism was our one way ticket out of Norristown.

The last game of the year was always the "Turkey Bowl" on Thanksgiving Day when Norristown played the rival town of Upper Merion. Everyone in the entire area was there—kids from both schools, their families, local business owners and the news stations. Any and everyone who loved high school football. The stadium seats were at capacity and people had to stand around the entire field behind the gate. This was the largest crowd I had ever played in front of. I'll never forget the beautiful energy of that moment and I also remember coming out of the locker room and heading onto the field. I looked over to the right and saw the guy who came by the house to sell my mom life insurance. He wished me luck and said he would be rooting for me. My head coach constantly reminded me throughout the season to only run north and south and I struggled to do it because my whole game was to "shake and bake." In other words, make a few moves to make people miss and score a touchdown just like Nimmy taught me. As a football player, you either have it or you don't and a coach that messes with your talent is not doing his team any favors. I was focused on getting to the next level and heard there were college scouts from the University of Miami in the stands.

It was the 4th quarter, and we were winning 7-0 when I started to feel this strange focus in my brain. My body became lighter and the little hairs on the back of my neck stood up. Just then, the opposing team's quarterback dropped back. I had my eyes on the receiver to the right and I started moving in his direction then, the tight end started crossing towards me in the middle. I stepped forward and slightly to the right. Things suddenly went into slow motion as I stepped in front of the receiver and boom! Interception. Here is a link so you can watch the play on YouTube. Start the video at 27:00

https://www.youtube.com/watch?v=NT9sOejYUIY

I caught the ball three yards back in the end zone and ran that sucker from end to end. It's still one of the longest documented touchdowns in the State of Pennsylvania. The whole stadium gave me a standing ovation and screamed and shouted my name as I ran to the sidelines very winded.

My childhood friend and teammate, Stephen Mccall made an amazing play on third down. He split the offensive lineman and cut straight through to the back field and tackled the running back for a loss. His play made it fourth and goal. I remember the words of the sports announcer on the video replay vividly, "The Eagles are coming pouring in on Rowinsky but I think they have to throw on this fourth and sixth. It's the play of the game to date with 7:51 left, fourth down and goal from the sixth, Lewinsky looking into the endzone—INTERCEPTED by Bazemore! Lenny Bazemore the SPEEDSTER. He might go all the way! Jeff Rowinsky, Jerry Hearn, trying to catch him—GOOD! BYE! 103-yard interception return for a touchdown! That's what makes Lenny Bazemore a great athlete! And what a disappointment for the Vikings knocking on the door as Lenny Bazemore intercepts it, the big play comes back to haunt the Vikings again. Later in that game, they said "He's going to be a great college player too."

The next morning, I woke up and walked to the store to pick up the newspaper. I'm not sure if kids still do this but, it'd be a shame if they don't—to wake up the next morning after crushing a game, there's such a thrill in seeing your name in print, announcing to the world that you did something great. It's the recognition that really makes a kid start to understand their value and self-worth. I would imagine the kids nowadays just log on to see if it's online, lol.

Right there where they talked about my play, that insane 103-yard interception return for a touchdown to win the game, my coach was quoted as saying, "I'm not saying Lenny did the wrong thing, but I wish he would've done a touchback."

Woah.

I had to read it again.

"I'm not saying Lenny did the wrong thing, but..."

But what man?

You gotta be kidding me. The wrong thing? But? I couldn't believe it. From my perch at the top of the world, I came right back down to the streets of Norristown, and I was devastated. Didn't I win him and his team the game? Didn't I try my hardest to use my best judgment? And wasn't I just a sensitive high school kid battling depression?

All I wanted was for that father figure to be proud of me, but instead I just felt like I did something wrong. I could have been so much better as an athlete had Coach Grove allowed me to be me, to allow my God-given abilities, critical thinking and decision-making skills to shine. I always respected him and cared for him but that year, I think we would have won every game if he would have just let me and my childhood friends do what we knew we could do.

In Norristown, there are only a handful of opportunities for kids to get out. The first is that you get good grades, get a scholarship or have decent parents that help you go to college, and you get out. The second is you're good at sports, get a scholarship that way, and you get out.

Other ways that you can grow in Norristown is you can go to a community college and transfer to a 4-year school or get a job. Otherwise, you get a job at a family business after high school or at a place where a family member works or some other place where you start at the bottom and work your way up the ladder. And you basically stay in the Norristown area and you pretty much live out the rest of your days there. If you are lucky, then maybe you can take your family on a vacation to the Jersey shore once or twice a year. Maybe even the Poconos or Disney in Florida once or twice in a lifetime but if you're looking for major growth, especially in terms of wealth and culture, I believe you have to go outside of Norristown to experience it.

I knew that football was my way out. I knew I was going to get a scholarship. I had stacks and stacks of letters from major Division 1 Colleges from all across the country that filled up half of my bedroom. When my childhood friends, Jason Duff, Darrell Moses, Marc Zaczkiewicz, Shawn Chatman, Curt Henning, Rob Horton, Johnny Carbone and Kem Johnson (A friend and Spiritual Advisor) to name a few, would come over, they'd joke and ask who wrote to me that week.

And here's the cool part: all these major universities were sending me letters asking me to visit their campus, they sent information about their schools including programs and, you know, calendars of cheerleaders and stuff. It was very enticing. And the school that caught my attention for many reasons was the University of Pittsburgh. It was close enough to home so my mom could see me play. The other thing that lured me in was that Dan Marino and Tony Dorsett, both wrote me personal letters and called me on the phone a few times. How mind blowing is that for a high school player? Dan Marino was a quarterback for the Miami Dolphins, (my cousin Izek Tuggle's favorite team,) and Tony Dorsett was a running back for the Dallas Cowboys. They were prominent stars in the NFL and they both attended Pitt.

I was invited to go visit the university and explore what that option would look like, but my family just didn't have the time or money to make the trip happen. Although I felt discouraged, there was always hope when you know how to look for it.

My girlfriend Kathy's mom and dad attended Saint Mary's College and the University of Notre Dame respectively, so after a conversation about Pitt playing Notre Dame that season, they were kind enough to take me to visit the university because the coaches gave me 3 extra tickets to the game. I was able to walk through the locker room, meet the players and walk the field. I knew instantly that I wanted to go to school there. I knew it was a fit for me because It felt so fucking good to be there. There were other national recruits in the room, and we were getting to know each other while eating different types of sandwiches including hoagies, a Philadelphia favorite. We were drinking soda and just chatting away, all while sizing each other up. It was a surreal experience! I was on a major college campus and still felt like a little high school football player, because on TV everyone and everything seemed so much larger.

Right before the game started, some of the coaches came to get us so we could tour the locker room as the players were getting ready for their game. We walked in and there he was, running back Craig "Ironhead" Hayward (Heisman finalist.) He was getting ready to put on his shoulder pads. I was standing there facing him when he said, "I know what you're thinking Lenny but, you can do this shit. Just come in and do what you've been doing all your life." I thanked him and a few steps away, I said "What's up" to Louis Riddick, an amazing football player who we played against in high school. He went to Pennridge High before attending Pitt, played pro and spent some time on the Raiders in 1998. He is one of my favorite broadcasters for ESPN. Mr. Riddick's analytical mind along with the knowledge of playing the game is why he is one of the best at what he does. On TV, the players looked massive, but there in that locker room, a lot of them were about the same size as me. It gave me this sudden confidence that helped me to believe that I really could make this dream happen. I had a real, solid chance to get out of Norristown by using my God-given talent. I will never forget that feeling. It was very meaningful to me and it felt like my body was filled with little bursts of energy on the inside and goose bumps all over on the outside. It was a highly combustible feeling and I literally felt like I could have walked on air if I tried. I was about to become something I dreamt about since I was a kid. I made sure that I took my time experiencing every single emotion while I was there because I knew it was a once in a lifetime moment. And as I walked onto the field, I experienced gratefulness. I thanked God for the opportunity because in that moment, I knew that everything I went through up to that point was going to be left behind. The pain, the abandonment, the lack of guidance and fatherly love. The depression and my old life would be in the past and my future was going to be amazing. The stadium was packed. It felt like I was born to be there. They let me walk on the turf and up into the stands where my girlfriend and her parents were seated. Seeing all those people in the stadium gave me more goosebumps because one day they would be cheering for me when I scored touchdowns or made interceptions. A coach came up and put a lanyard game day pass around my neck and said that if I wanted anything from the concession stand, all I had to do was show the pass and I could have it.

During the game, as I watched my future Pitt team play against the Fighting Irish, all I could think about was how blessed I was to be afforded the opportunity to play college football, get an education for free, and be the first person in my immediate family to go to school. I was going to make them all proud. Hell, even my uncles were pestering me, talking about how I was going to be in the NFL and they couldn't wait to watch me on TV. Funny thing is, I'm a Raiders fan and Tim Brown was a star player for Notre Dame in that game against Pitt. He was eventually drafted by my favorite team so; I had a chance to watch his entire career. I watched Louis Riddick play too. I used to wonder what it would have felt like if I ended up playing ball on my favorite team in the NFL with Tim Brown and Louis Riddick.

I was on my way to playing college football at a major school. I guess Kathy took note of all of this during our trip because when we got home it became apparent to me that she did not want me to leave. Suddenly she was crying and saying, "Please don't leave me and don't you dare leave me." It became this mental tug of war. I knew that I needed to get out of Norristown. I knew that I was gifted and that I had what it would take to achieve the dream of becoming a college football player. I wanted to financially take care of my mother in the way that she deserved. And I wanted to prove that I didn't need a competent father figure in order to be successful.

Kathy's constant nagging created this hostile and traumatic time for me because I obviously didn't want to leave her, but I knew I had to get out. So, I made the tough decision to block her out as much as I could. I was ready to sign the letter of intent to attend the University of Pittsburgh to play football and get an education. I started mentally preparing to leave Norristown. I was so fucking close to my dream.

One day I was walking through the halls when I ran into Kathy.

"Can you please tell Tony Buffa to leave me alone? He keeps squeezing my ass in gym class."

She was asking for help because she was being sexually harassed and groped by Tony. He was verbally abusive as well. She told me that he would constantly chastise her about dating a black guy and that he would ask her to break up with me and give him a chance instead. So, I told her that she needed to report him to the gym teacher. I didn't know this guy or know what he even looked like. All I heard was that he and his entire family were black belts in martial arts. His older brother, Jerry Buffa, was a football teammate and friend of mine, so why was it my problem?

A few days later and after the final bell, Tony approached me by the gym on school property. He was apparently jealous that my girlfriend turned down his advances so he set out to come after me. I would imagine in his sick mind that he may have thought if he knocked the popular and well-liked football guy off his high horse then he would be the man. His premeditated anger and demeanor was unsettling. He looked and acted like a rabid dog. The fool came looking for trouble that day.

"What the fuck, man? I heard you got a problem with me," "he said."

"Nah man," I responded. "I don't even know who the fuck you are," and that should have been the end of it!

I was an athletic 5'11 195 lbs of solid muscle and Tony, this scrawny white boy got all up in my face, acting tough. I kept my cool though, because this little clown didn't mean shit to me. I was on the cusp of leaving him and every other punk just like him in the dust on my way to the big leagues and I didn't need this shit.

In a fit of rage and in the blink of an eye, Tony spit in my face and smacked me with his right hand. A little bit of snot came out of my nose and settled onto my cheek. That sometimes happened when I got tackled in football because of the force.

Somehow, by the grace of God, I managed to keep my cool.

"Look man, whatever," I said, as I tried to leave by walking out to the parking lot. He followed me and started calling me all kinds of demeaning names. He ran in front of me and did some karate move and I ducked. I reacted by punching him in the jaw and then watched him drop to the ground. This bitch ass motherfucking tough guy talking all that shit was now headed to the hospital.

I was dragged into the office of one of my football coaches. You see at that time, Coach Joseph Fabrizio was also the school's disciplinarian. I frantically tried to tell my coach that I was defending myself, telling him how Tony spit in my face, hit me, used threatening verbal abuse and tried to hit me again. I was rightfully defending myself after being the so-called bigger person by walking away. He didn't seem to believe me. I was so scared because I thought, "How could my football coach not believe me?" As a black person, I also wondered if I had rights that would protect me or was my blackness going to be a disadvantage in this situation. I remember almost passing out after being in a state of panic because I didn't know what was going to happen to me. I was so frightened and felt this huge sense of loneliness and darkness come over me. I didn't want to go to prison but thought I would. I was never again in my life as scared as I was on the day the cops showed up at my house, read my rights, placed me in handcuffs and arrested me. Later, when my mother went to see Coach Fabrizio, he broke her heart by telling her that I would never play football again. Which I thought was coldblooded.

Let's hit replay.

Tony, an affluent white kid spit in my face (assault,) slapped me (assault,) and then tried to hit me again (assault.) I ducked out of the way and punched him (self defense.)

Tony spent a couple of days in the hospital. Ultimately, he was fine and even though he was the assailant, he literally walked away from it all. No injuries, no charges and no arrest. For a few days, the reality of it all was too much for me to mentally handle. I felt like my brain was losing it because it convinced me that it was all just a bad dream. But then I snapped out of my delusion and realized it was a white kid's story versus a black kid's story. It's not that hard to figure out that I was born a winner and 5 seconds later, I was going to lose.

I was thankful there were a few witnesses when I showed up to the Magisterial District Court for a preliminary hearing which would determine if there was enough evidence to continue on to trial. But before the hearing began, this white lady came rushing up to me, my mom, and my uncle Nabop.

"Are you the Bazemores'?" she asked frantically.

"Yes," we said. Mind you, we were all uneducated regarding the court system.

"I didn't tell you this," she said. "You didn't hear this from me. But you do not want to have a preliminary hearing. You need to waive your right to the preliminary hearing, and you want to take it right to court. Trust me. That's what you need to do. It's your best chance of getting out of this."

"Are you sure?" my mom asked.

"It's the only way to beat it." She spoke.

And so, we went in and I waived my right to the hearing.

I received a notification from the school letting me know that I was immediately expelled due to my behavior on school property and the resulting arrest and court case. I was told that I was not allowed to return.

And then it got worse.

The University of Pittsburgh revoked its offer and scholarship.

Kathy got what she wanted. I wasn't going anywhere anytime soon.

And then came the rock bottom part. I had to tell my Mom Mom.

I went to visit her soon after it happened and sat her down at the kitchen table. I told her everything. She started crying, and it was the worst thing I had ever seen or heard up until that point. My poor Grandma.

"Baby, you broke Mom Mom's heart," she cried. "I thought you were going to go to college to get a degree and play that football."

And she cried some more. If her heart was broken, my heart was pulverized. I could hardly keep it together. But I had to. Because I knew this couldn't be the end.

"Mom Mom don't worry. I'm going to get a college education. I'm going to get a degree one day. I'm going to be successful. I promise that will make you proud."

SEVEN

Trials, Tribulations, and a Baby Born

The air was stuffy when I woke up the morning after telling Mom Mom what happened. I opened the window hoping it would be cool out, but that Norristown air flowed right in and felt even more stifling. Everything felt still, what I imagined it felt like after a bomb went off but during that split second right before anyone realized what happened. Life felt different. The people felt different. Norristown felt different. I felt different. I still had to get out. But after years of fighting, fighting and fighting—after years of just wanting to do good and be somebody, I felt like I had been beaten to the ground and I feared I might not have enough left in me to achieve even one percent of those lofty goals and ambitions of mine. And for a while, I was at risk of becoming just another impoverished black kid stuck in the hood he grew up in—a damn statistic. Similar to the Allen Iverson story but he was fortunate to get another chance to go on to be a star at Georgetown University. Thank God because he was iconic in every way. One of the greatest to ever play the game. We all watched him change the game in addition to changing the way the world embraced black culture. He was just being himself but influenced every race and culture to be down with the brown. We all owe "Bubba Chuck", a big thank you for persevering and being resilient.

I was alone with no support at that courthouse for the hearing of my life and no witnesses showed up. I had no idea what was going on. I was so confused because I was facing fifteen years in prison. The fear of losing my freedom because a white dude lied after he assaulted me was the devil's work. I am so thankful that my public defender was able to plead it down and I was lucky to only receive just one year of probation at the trial. It had to be the Good Lord at work that literally saved my ass that day. Part of being on probation was having steady employment. I got a part-time job working at a deli and I was required to do a piss test every month at Montgomery County Adult Probation Office in Norristown, Pa, which was very demeaning because I was treated like shit by my white probation officer.

They despised me and every time I had to walk through their office, they all stared at me like a was fucking criminal with no future. Threats of sending me to prison to ruin my life were constant. There was no compassion or respect. In their eyes, I was nothing more than a bad person who committed a crime. I was already depressed but it made me feel almost worthless. In retrospect, I am thankful for the experience because I was drinking heavily and doing a lot of drugs to ease the pain. The urine tests were conducted every single month and if I tested positive for anything at all, I was going straight to prison. So, I stayed clean and that actually helped me before I spiraled down the point of no return. At work, I was promoted from cashier to the kitchen and man did I learn how to make the best reuben sandwiches (still one of my favorites,) and since I was only two classes shy of graduating, Norristown High School allowed me to return to complete those classes, which I liked to call the thirteenth grade. I was dealing with deep depression and embarrassment at this point but continued to give it everything I had. While walking to my locker one afternoon, I ran into Kathy who was reading a note from this dude and ex-teammate, Mike Caroll. I snatched the letter and ran out of the school towards my car in the parking lot. He wrote to her, "I want to see you tonight, I love you," all this bullshit! Kathy was running behind my back with him and now she was running after me in the parking lot yelling that she loved me, and I realized, I just couldn't do it anymore. I dropped out and opted to get my GED instead. I did the community college schtick for a year catching a ride three times a week with my friend Charles Interrante but it was too immature for me—the parties, the level of intellect—none of it matched where I was trying to get to. The bar was too low and the depression was too intense, so I stopped going.

To make it worse, some of my friends who were not as talented went off to college and played ball; some of them stayed home. And then I realized that for those who went off to college, I was placed in the category of "those who stayed home." And damn that hurt. I overestimated my talent and underestimated other people's drive and discipline. I lost a lot by this time in my life—my scholarship, my potential career, my girlfriend, my pride. I was arrested, charged and prosecuted for a crime that was done against me. Every damn thing that mattered to me, was lost.

Probation ended after a year and I was still living with my mom and JB, so I'd go work at whatever job I could find. Then I would hangout with my boys, Rob Horton and Brian Harrison to play basketball, drive around in Brian's 5.0 Mustang GT or just chill, get drunk and high then come home at one, two in the morning just to do it all over again the next day. I also hung out with my friend Henry Racich a lot because he always put a smile on my face when I was bummed out. We would go dancing at Touché or Popcorns nightclub. Go swimming at his grandma's house and sing Karaoke at a bar on Ridge Pike. There were a bunch of kids who were doing the same thing—taking advantage of living with mom and dad and just coasting through life. I threw a lot of parties in those two years after high school, attracting many types of people since I was so popular in high school and the surrounding communities. And as cool as that was, it was just two years of craziness—sex, drugs, rock and roll, hip hop and alcohol, you name it.

Kathy attended Seton Hall University until transferring to St. Joe's in Philadelphia. Obviously, I didn't learn my lesson and ended up dating her on and off. But, after experiencing all of her antics, all the controlling and dragging me down instead of building me up, it just made me feel like she was trying to trap me and I didn't feel like settling down anymore. I decided it was better to fool around and just live my life for me—no one else.

This period of transition in my life offered a lot of low paying jobs, most of which I'd get sick of quickly because I knew in my heart and soul, they weren't helping me achieve some of the goals I imagined. Goals such as owning a home, being able to provide for myself and traveling the world. You see, those goals were the more present goals in my mind, whereas my childhood dreams of owning that mansion on the hill and flying in a private jet—I still held on to those goals, but at this point in my life, they seemed unachievable.

One of the jobs I held was at Armen Cadillac as a Gofer (someone who performs deliveries, errands and other special tasks.) All of my friends were getting cars, meanwhile I had a job but no car. So, I called my biological father, Hampton, and said, "Hey, you know, I have never asked you for anything. I need you to cosign for me so I can get this loan for $2,500 so I can buy a car." He drove up to help me sign with the bank but there was no conversation about what was going on in my life. He never seemed to care. He just said, "make sure you pay on time" and he jumped in his car and left. It's not like I was looking forward to spending quality time with him anyway. He was not interested in a meaningful relationship with me. I was thankful for his help but I felt like he owed me since he never paid child support.

My loan payments were around $80 per month and I was able to make them on time. But then there came a period towards the end of the loan. Maybe three or four months where money was tight and paying the loan just wasn't feasible. I thought the repo man would show up and just take the car, but they never did. Come to find out, Hampton took care of the payments when I failed to. We never discussed it. I guess he did what he needed to do to protect his own credit.

So, while he was not there for me in any other way, I will give him credit where a little credit is due; he pulled through on that loan, and I appreciated it.

Another gig I had was selling area rugs and carpet. And after a month or two of doing that, I worked for a Japanese anime toy store. Got sick of that too. As you can imagine, neither of those jobs paid much. So, I went over to this restaurant and bar in King of Prussia called Houlihan's because it was the hottest spot around at that time. And the only job they had available was as a dishwasher. I took it and man; I was one hell of a dishwasher. You needed sunglasses because of the shine emanating from my clean dishes. But of course, just like the rug and toy stores, I got sick of it—quick. So, I went to the manager and said, "Listen, I appreciate the job, but I want to work my way up to bouncer."

"No problem, she said. "You're on the radar."

After about two weeks, she called me into the office and asked if I could work as a bouncer that next Sunday because she had to fire one of the current bouncers.

"Absolutely," I said.

"Good, here is the list for the attire." She replied.

So next Sunday, I showed up in my penny loafers, khakis, and my seersucker shirt, ready to do some bouncing. I was looking handsome. I debuted and worked by the DJ booth for about a month and eventually worked my way up to the front door. I'll never forget Houlihan's. They made one hell of a French onion soup and the place always smelled like beer. And to be the bouncer of a bar, especially at that time in 1990—man, that made you the shit. So even though it wasn't paying enough to make these big dreams come true, it still satisfied the part of me that was looking for a good time with pay.

And all these Au pairs who came in from Europe. Girls from

Norway, Finland, England and France. To meet these beautiful women from across the world was enlightening. It helped me to realize that I didn't have to be with plain old girls like Kathy. That wasn't what I had to settle for. I could do better.

Meanwhile, an old teammate and childhood friend of mine named Kenny, went off to follow one of those rare paths out of Norristown by going to college and afterwards, becoming an assistant junior college football coach down in North Carolina. He came knocking on the front door one day.

"Come on, man," I remember him saying. "You're too talented of an athlete to be laying on your mom's couch. Come play with us down at the school. Get back on track. Make something of yourself."

I couldn't believe it. After a few years of constant depression and being convinced that I was stuck in Norristown forever—it was almost as if the sky had cleared and the sun started shining because there was hope again.

Hope.

Funny word, hope. It derives from the Dutch words hoop and hopen, and from the German word hoffen, all of which share the root for the word "curve." In other words, headed in another direction. And the Greek equivalent, elpis, means expectation, trust, confidence. So really, an expectation, trust, and confidence that one will head in another direction. Something I most certainly didn't expect when I was deep in my state of having no hope. How could I, when all of my opportunities had been stripped from me? And after all that I had lost?

I wasn't about to lose this opportunity, too.

I started working out like a mad man and running. I stopped drinking and getting high and replaced that with activities that would make me healthier, stronger and happier. I was ready to roll and maybe, just maybe, if I could get back to my star athleticism, college would be a breeze and I'd still have a shot at the NFL or getting a job in professional sports.

Just before I was ready to leave, my mom came up to me.

"Hey baby. I know you're about to go off and play college ball and I'm very proud of you," she said, "but I wanted you to know that Kathy is pregnant."

"Well, it ain't mine," I said, with the vocal equivalent of putting my foot down. "I broke up with her four months ago."

"Baby, I'm so sorry but that's the problem. She just never told you and she is four months pregnant."

I couldn't believe it. Here I was, on the cusp of yet another life changing opportunity and it's being threatened. And yet again, another opportunity being sabotaged by Kathy.

So, I called her up and asked her what the fuck was going on.

"I'm pregnant," she said.

"No shit! Well, I'm about to leave to play college ball and get an education," I said.

"Well then , you're leaving me and the baby."

And that hit me right in the fatherhood chin.

We have all heard that story before. Athlete shows promise, the girl tries to trap him or worse, she tries to tame him and ultimately that can destroy a man.

But, after all that JB put me through in my life. After all, Hampton put me through. After a life of terrible father figures, that statement of leaving us was hard to hear. But it was also eye-opening. You see, I wanted to be a father one day. That was part of the American Dream I thought about, but I was nowhere close to being ready to hear those words yet. That big house on the hill I always envisioned, it wasn't full of parties, sexy women, fancy cars, and whatever else people imagine bachelors do. You see, it was going to be filled with family and love. And money. Shit loads of money.

But I never wanted Kathy to be the mother of any of my children. I knew she wouldn't bring excellence to my house on the hill. I knew the private jet with champagne and caviar would look nothing like Nick Kimball and Dominique Deveraux if she was onboard.

But I refused to be a deadbeat to my child like my two fathers were to me.

And so, I stayed. I got a job working third shift at this busted gas station to contribute to the cost of raising our baby.

I had a life altering decision to make and as a young man, I hadn't yet experienced living outside of Norristown. Just like "Easy on Me" by Adele, "I was still a child, didn't get the chance to feel the world around me. I had no time to choose what I chose to do." I wanted to see what was out there beyond the state of Pennsylvania and to evolve into manhood naturally and on my terms. Right then and there, I chose to sacrifice the last little bit of happiness I had left inside of me and dedicate it to my son.

Just to be sure, I asked for a blood test and her father Frank walked me down the front pathway of their house. He firmly placed his hand on the back of my neck and said, "What are you talking about a blood test for? The kid is yours."

Mind you, this was a loving, quiet and gentle man who was now gripping me by the back of the neck asking what are you talking about a blood test for? "I want you to drop this subject and I don't want to hear about it again."

So, I dropped it.

Why? Because at the end of the day, through all this bullshit, despite all this bullshit, I'm an honorable man. My mother raised me well—and watching JB taught me—that if I wanted to be something one day, I needed to be responsible. Although I needed to do what was necessary to survive, I would still have to be respectful, honest, conscientious, and upright. I needed to be moral. So that's what I decided I'd do. When my child turned eighteen, maybe then I'd get the blood test. But for now, I was going to do what was right. I wasn't going to be like Hampton. And I most certainly wasn't going to be like JB. I was going to be Leonard Arnett Bazemore—the guy who would sacrifice his own life for his child.

In 1991, my son, Devon Arnett, was born at 7 pounds 11 ounces, just like his daddy. They let me cut the umbilical cord and I was the first person to hold him. The feeling I experienced in those moments is hard to describe. It was heavenly—to see this baby that I created, this tiny human being. If I had to put a descriptor on it, I'd say it was joyful elation times one hundred. And all I wanted was for him to be healthy.

By no choice of my own, I became a father at 22-years-old.

To hold the baby. To feed the baby. To give the baby a name and his start in life. It was unparalleled to any experience I ever had. We were going to give him a good life, a good head start. He was going to have it better than I did.

EIGHT

Life in the Blink of an Eye

Uncle Mann, my mother's twin brother, had just gotten married. It was one hell of a wedding reception at the Norristown Carver Center and after the sun went down, me, my cousins, and some friends, headed down to a bar called the Gold Star, a place where my mom was a bartender part-time. A lot of people congratulated me because my son was born just two months prior. We were out celebrating life by getting high and drinking forties, you know, having a dope ass time. Hip hop was massive on the scene and we listened to Public Enemy, A Tribe Called Quest, Nice and Smooth, Special ED, Run DMC, Big Daddy Kane and LL Cool J. Everyone in the hood was celebrating our African heritage by wearing medallions on a necklace in the shape of the African continent, wearing African colors on T-shirts and such. It was empowering. It felt like we were more connected than ever as black folk our age, strangers or not. So, Ironically, I see this dude laying up against his car windshield and I say, "What up, my brotha? What's good?"

So, this crab in a barrel says, "Yo! fuck you, nut."

"Who are you callin' nut?" I asked.

"Man, you ain't shit."

I had no clue who this fool was, as he got all up in my face. My sister Tara and our friend Mona Lisa (real name Lisa Navarro) came up and said, "Don't fight him Lenny, don't fight him, that's Lark Ramsey."

I still didn't know who this dude was.

They said he was fresh out of jail. A real tough guy!

I turned to walk away and boom—no warning—dude punched me in my face. I looked at him and he knew he fucked up! I was able to hit him a few times, grabbed him, slammed his head into the wall, flipped him over and started beating his ass into the ground. Just then, someone came up and stabbed me in the back twice. Several people there said it was his sister Felicia.

Red. Everywhere. Suddenly I was four again, holding Nimmy's hand as I was rushed through the streets to the hospital.

Lark went to his car to get his gun, but my boys rushed me to the emergency room.

Blood gushing everywhere. Spurting out of me.

I remember my friend Rob Horton putting pressure on my wounds and screaming, "Don't die, Lenny! Don't die!"

Next thing I knew I was in the ER being examined by this Doctor, poking around in my back and cleaning out my wounds.

"Thank God you've got so much muscle back here," she said. "If you didn't, she could have severed your spine."

That was a lot to deal with. It didn't quite sit in my consciousness because of the gravity of hearing it.

"You're lucky to be walking," she said.

They stitched up both wounds, gave me some Tylenol—no hard drugs—and sent me on my way. The pain was unbearable.

The next few weeks were just as traumatic for me. See, you have to understand, being stabbed and nearly dying from it—that changes you. It gave me severe anxiety and induced panic attack after panic attack. I was afraid to leave the house, not only because those fools were still out there, but because if that could happen on a joyous night, what would happen to me any other night?

More panic attacks.

Not to mention the physical deterioration that occurred, difficulty walking, sleeping, taking a shower and bending over to tie my shoes. After twenty-two years of being physically capable, not being able to move around freely scared the shit of me.

More panic attacks.

But at the time, I didn't even know they were called panic attacks. All I thought was, Fuck, life can be a bitch because I was almost killed.

My cousin Reggie Roberts was a cop at the time and we knew who these two were and we had a bunch of witnesses. I could have pressed charges on both of them, but I chose not to. The streets can be funny sometimes and you need to know how to maneuver in them if you want to survive.

About three weeks after the stabbing, I was walking by the BJ Lounge near Spruce and Powell Streets and some dude was on the payphone outside; he kind of turned and said, "Yo, what's up Lenny?" I said, "Yo, what's up?" With my head down, I kept walking to my mom's house. I cut through the parking lot near Jules Sweet Shop and the dude that was on the payphone followed me and screams, "Yo Lenny!"

I turned around and it was Lark Ramsey with his gun pointed at my head.

In that moment, there was no time to think, there was no hesitation.

I shouted "Look man, if you gonna shoot me, shoot me! If not, fuck you."

I turned and kept walking. And he did the same.

What Lark didn't see though, was that I was shaking to my core.

I cried all the way home. I cried for hours and thanked God over and over again that I wasn't just murdered.

About a week later, my friends got me out of the house. We went down to the basketball courts on Oak Street where everybody in the hood would watch everyone else play basketball. I got out of the car, walked over to the gate, and the first person—I mean literally, the first person I saw was Lark leaning against the fence.

I had the opportunity to walk away because he didn't see me. I could have been a coward and disappeared or went back to my mommy's house like a little boy and lived in fear for the rest of my life.

But that's not the Norristown way. That's not how we handle shit. Like I said, Nimmy prepared me for the streets! I wanted to face him. I wanted to be resilient and I honestly wanted peace, but part of me wanted to beat his motherfucking ass in front of everyone. He should have never fucked with me in the first place.

He had a 100% chance to shoot me in my face in that parking lot that night and get away with it. There was absolutely no one around. It would have been done so quickly. I would have been dead. Body cold and six feet underground with my family mourning my loss. He had the perfect chance. But he didn't shoot.

So, I went up to him.

"Yo," I said. "We cool?"

"Yeah," he said. "We cool."

I already had mad respect in the streets, but after getting stabbed and standing up to Lark with his gun in my face, it basically solidified my street credibility. (He is currently serving up to 70 years in a Pennsylvania Prison for an unrelated crime.)

But in private, man, it fucked with me. Physical trauma and mental trauma because I ain't about that street life man. I was trying my best to get out of the hood and that shit doesn't just go away. Since there was a baby involved, Kathy and I got back together. I was a father of a two-month-old so I needed to shake this shit off. I was struggling to make ends meet but still, I knew I had to get out of Norristown one day if I wanted to survive and achieve my American Dream for me and my family. I didn't know what the fuck I was going do to get ahead so, I did what any decent young man would do, I just focused on raising my son.

I was still working third shift at the gas station. I'd come home, watch my son during the day until his mom would come and pick him up so I could go get some sleep before work. Eventually we got him into daycare with Ms. Pat, the sweet neighbor up the street who watched some of the neighborhood kids. Ms. Pat, if you're reading this, thank you for taking care of my son when he was a baby. You were educational, you infused his life with sweetness at such a young age. You were fundamental in providing that first step. Thank you.

And you know, I tried to make it work with Kathy for the sake of our baby, but she was intolerable and too controlling, focused only on small-town life in terms of getting married, buying a house and things of that nature instead of achieving bigger goals like seeing the world. We were both so young and I was curious about traveling and wanted to experience other cultures around the globe.

On Wednesday nights down on City Line Avenue there was this club called Networks. They had good music, the girls were cute, and they had cheap drinks. So, me and my friend Ryan Henning headed down on a Wednesday. And when I was getting out of his car, I saw this woman getting out of her friend's car. And I mean, it was just like in the movies. We both did the classic double take at the same time, and she was pretty, so I said, "What up." She said "Hey", and we all walked in at the same time. Me and my boy headed to the bar to get drinks and about 30 minutes later, I looked up and saw her on the dance floor, standing there with a light shining down on her, as if she was standing there waiting for me.

I walked up to her and said, "Do you want to dance?"

"Yeah, sure," she said.

"What are you doing just standing here?" I asked.

And without missing a beat, she said, "Waiting on you."

So, we danced for a bit. Her name was Danielle, and she

wasn't just pretty. She was kind and sweet. She said "Give me your number, so I gave it to her. Well, the number to my mom's house.

"You didn't write it down?" I said.

She responded, "I'll remember it."

"You sure?" I asked.

"Trust me, I'll remember you."

A few days later, I got a call, and we started talking.

We made plans but for whatever reason they fell through and we kind of lost touch.

It wasn't a big deal, though, because I had so many other preoccupations as a young father trying to provide for his son.

One Thursday night in 1992, I was in King of Prussia at this bar called Gators. I was walking back from the bathroom when I saw Danielle come through the front door.

"Oh shit, it's you!" I said. "Who are you with?"

I noticed she was with this guy James Jones that I grew up with. I said, "I see you're with my man" and started walking away, but she started walking with me.

"Ain't you talking to James?" I asked.

"No, I'm with you."

After we sat down and started talking, Danielle said,

"I lost you once. I'm not losing you again."

I wanted to make sure that I was respecting her and that I was also respecting James as well. I try not to encroach on another person in that way.

From there, Danielle and I were together every week, all the time. It was hot and heavy, and we fell in love quickly. She was such a joy to be with.

And after ten months, we decided to elope and didn't tell anyone.

We went up to New York to hang out with Danielle's lifelong friend Heather and her boyfriend Calvin. And at the end of the weekend, they decided to come down to Pennsylvania to attend our Justice of the Peace wedding.

We went and got our marriage certificate, then a judge

married us. We did it all with paper clips for rings with Heather and Calvin Pierce (who are now married,) as a bridesmaid and best man. We secretly sealed the deal and I was married at 23!

Our honeymoon was at the Chili's restaurant on Chestnut Street, University City, Philly and right below it was a strip club. Calvin and I went outside for air and found our way to the club to get a beer for a post wedding-bachelor party. And it truly was a great party for about ten minutes because our ladies came down and we got caught. All in good fun, though.

Things were good. I was playing house and had this new wife that I loved. The relationship was terrific, and we were building a little life together. Things were starting to look up again, as if I was over the hurdles life was throwing at me.

In 1993, Danielle told me she was pregnant, and I couldn't believe it. This time however, I was happy because she was my wife.

In 1991, when Kathy told me she was pregnant, I couldn't believe that was happening to me. I was in no position to be a father and was getting ready to leave and play junior college football. I imagined having this amazing career and then, when I was ready, at a time of my choosing, I'd become a father. All in all, I am proud of the decision I made to put our child before my hopes and dreams. With Danielle, it was a different feeling. I was elated when she told me she was pregnant even though it meant that I was now going to have two young children that I wasn't ready for. All in all, it was an incredible feeling to find out that I was going to have another kid and even though it wasn't planned, I was looking forward to building my family.

In 1993, Danielle and I made the decision to move me into her parents' home in Overbrook, Philadelphia on 63rd Street where she was already living. It was a surreal feeling when I left Norristown. It felt like I was taking the first step toward my goal of having the American Dream. I was checking off the boxes. I had a wife, and she loved my son from another woman. I had a plan to start saving money. And in a way, I had a father figure in

Danielle's dad, Big Mike. He was a charismatic man who played college football at Villanova University, and I really looked up to him.

The desire to live in another man's home while being married to his daughter is absolutely fucking weird to me now. But, back then, I was a 23 year old trying to emulate another man. I watched every move he made so I could learn how to be a man. I was trying to learn the right way to take care of a family and at the end of the day, life was alright.

In 1994, after securing a decent job with health benefits, I needed a reliable car so I could get to work at the Glen Mill Schools where I was a security guard on the night shift, (the students called us Nightman.) I was able to save money by catching a ride with my friend John Thornton and a few other peers every night. I made an appointment at Springfield, Pa. Hyundai dealership to take advantage of a sale they were having. After adding up the money I saved, I still needed about $500 more for the down payment. I was running out of time because the sale was ending, so I called my #2 dad Hampton and he drove by to give me the money. But that was about it. There was no emotional connection. There was no love or even getting out of his car. It was a quick, how is everyone doing and then a simple handing over the motherfucking money. I imagine he may have thought that it was the least he could do since he was able to save all his money for himself. We never had anything close to a real relationship or connection. All I know is that he never came around to spend time with me to shoot hoops, play catch, talk about life or any other essential needs of a man. He never helped my mother to financially care for me. He still doesn't really know me and I have no idea who he really is and I'm finally ok with that after all these years. He just never bothered. I'm still incredibly grateful for the $500 that he gave me to buy another car but, if you think about the grand scheme of things—in terms of a father being responsible for a child he created, he is a major failure and could have done a whole lot more. He could have given my mom a little money to care for me every now and again. That grown ass man failed me and it hurt for a very long time.

On October 5, 1994, we welcomed our beautiful daughter, Jordan Amara, into the world.

And the only challenge I found with fatherhood was financially. I was 25 years old and working at Glen Mills making $25K a year but I still managed to make sure my kids had a great life. There was plenty of adventure on a budget that we enjoyed. We would always find something cool to do in and around Philadelphia. Like going to the zoo or heading down to Penn's Landing for outdoor family concerts. We went to amusement parks, outlet stores and had water balloon fights on the lawn.

You see, that's the big difference between me and my two emotionally unavailable fathers. I realized that if you are a quality human, if you have good morals and values, if you genuinely want to be a good father and provide and protect your children, you will do it no matter what. You may not do everything right. Hell, you'll make a lot of mistakes. But if you spend time with them, and simply try to be a good dad and if you love your kids as much as you can, you will mean everything to them. The financial aspect of it all, sure, that was challenging. I couldn't buy everything my kids wanted. But I loved them more than anything in life and I made sure they had everything they needed. And, not to spoil the story but I have a great relationship with two out of the three, which ain't bad!

A little over 2 years after Jordan was born, Danielle told me she was pregnant again. And just the same, I was thrilled.

On December 11, 1997, we welcomed Alexis Laryn into the world. It took us two days to name her. Danielle's mother, Marsha, came in for a visit and she asked if we had decided on a name yet. I proudly said, "We named her Alexis," after the character in Dynasty. She laughed in my face and said, "Alexis? Well, that's good because that's the closest you'll ever get to having one." I know it's funny but it's really not! I looked at her as just another person who doubted me. Not to mention, she didn't want us together in the first place. You see, Danielle was mixed race. Her mother was black and her father white. Marsha let it be known that she would have preferred her daughter marry a white dude with no ambition versus a black guy like me with plenty of ambition.

Danielle was a great mother to our daughters, and my son Devon too. She valued respect and education, and we had plans to make sure they never experienced a childhood like mine. We wanted to do this parenting thing right.

Unfortunately, Danielle seemed comfortable staying at her parents' house for all those years. And I mean, saving the loot was nice, but at that point, we both were making enough money to get a decent apartment. I asked her on several occasions and even found a few suitable 2 and 3 bedrooms. They were big enough so that Devon had a place to sleep when he'd come over. But it was evident that Danielle didn't want to leave the sanctity of her parents' home. There was always a lame excuse. "There will be no one here to do the dishes, no one to clean the house." She would say.

Sometime in the year 2000 (Y2K), our marriage started to fall apart. I will never know why. I suspect the pressure of adulting made her cave. Some people just can't handle the responsibility of growing up and facing the world head on. Being a grown-up is actually really hard but what are you going to do? Not grow up? Not take responsibility for your own life? Live with your parents forever? Many people sabotage their future because of many different reasons. So, whatever the reason, we just weren't meant to be with each other for the long-term. She was a great mother at the time; I was a great father and we truly did love each other once. But our communication had become fraught and there were several attempts to salvage what we had. Not just for us, but for the kids. You see, I was determined to be there no matter what and to make sure my kids had a stable life. I knew that could still be possible if I wasn't married to their mother—I proved that with Kathy and Devon—but it would have been so much more comfortable if we could stay together.

Danielle entered some contest and won a night at this

romantic getaway called the Inn of the Dove in Bensalem, Pa, which she surprised me with. For whatever reason, unfortunately, I couldn't make it. And I later learned that was her last attempt at making our relationship work. So, when that night didn't happen, our relationship was dead in the water. Looking back on it, I am so fucking thankful because it's possible that another baby would have been conceived that night.

Despite the fragility of our relationship, I was determined to give our kids a stable life.

When Danielle's grandmother passed away, she left her home in Yeadon, Pa. to Danielle's mother Marsha and her siblings. And after years of saving and hustling, I was ready to buy a home. I approached her mom and said, "Hey, I want to keep the house in the family so I can one day give it to my daughters, your grand-daughters. I'll buy the house for fair market value so don't put it up for sale."

Within months, and after going through the whole mortgage process, I was just a few signatures away from owning my first house.

On that life changing day, ice cold Danielle told me she wasn't going to move in.

Huh? Did I hear that right?

"I'm not moving in, Lenny," she said. "I'm seeing someone else."

I couldn't believe what I was hearing. Turned out that Danielle had been seeing this white dude for a couple of months and her mother encouraged it. So, I made settlement on the house, collected my new keys, and went back to her parents' house so I could pack up my shit because they straight up kicked me out. That whole family knows how to keep dirty little secrets and knew what was going on behind my back. I was destroyed and crying as I hugged my 2 and 5 year old daughters. I told them that I loved them. I said that I would see them soon and kissed them goodbye.

The only place I could go that night was to my new home. Instead of moving in with my family, I moved in by myself. The house didn't have electricity or heat which reminded me of some nights while growing up in Norristown. I put all my bags and boxes in the living room, and I made a little bed on the floor with a pillow and some blankets. I put a log on the fireplace and just like that, I went from having a family to having a broken marriage and living in my new home with no heat all by myself. This was not how I imagined my American Dream would be.

NINE

Life Changing but not for the Better

I spent the next seven months getting 3 to 4 hours of sleep a night renovating that home in hopes of convincing Danielle to move in with the girls. I would work at night then drive to her parents house to watch my 2 year old daughter. At noon, I would place her in a wagon and we would walk a few blocks away to pick up Jordan from school. I would make their lunch and we would watch some kid shows. When their mother came home after work, she would come into the house and ignore me. She never wanted to talk about our separation. I was left in the dark with no answers.

I would kiss my daughters goodbye then jump in my car and drive 20 minutes to my house to do some renovations before going to sleep and doing it all over again. It was brutal on my mind, body and soul. I know some people are gonna say I'm crazy for that—for wanting to salvage a relationship with a cheater—but she was still the mother of two of my children. And when you grow up the way I did, in poverty, with a fantastic mother but two deadbeat dads, you do everything you can to make sure your children have a better childhood than you did. Of course, that's providing that you are still capable of empathy and not closed off to the world to protect yourself from ever being hurt again. Besides, I was 30 years old with 3 kids trying to figure out life and swallowing my pride to give my kids a safe stable home was my one goal.

Finally, after all that hard work and 7 long months later, the house was finished. What a great accomplishment because I learned all aspects of renovation. I was so proud of myself. One night on the way back home after visiting my mom in Norristown, I was driving down a street called City Line Ave. It separates Philadelphia and Bala Cynwyd, Pa. I looked over to the right and just happened to see the car that I purchased with the help of my father's $500 gift. It was a blue 1994 Hyundai Excel with tinted windows and custom rims parked next to a black Cadillac Eldorado in a parking lot. I drove over in my red Plymouth Voyager minivan and it was Danielle and her boyfriend talking. I pulled up and asked him to get out of the car so I could beat his ass for being a homewrecker. I was taken aback when I noticed that he was overweight and wasn't attractive at all. I thought to myself, "Damn, how in the world could she leave me for that mess!" I asked him again to get out of his car and he started crying and she asked me to leave him alone. I realized it wasn't worth it so I just left and went home. Turns out they were breaking up and after Danielle left the other man, she and the girls were willing to move into the family home.

It's never easy and since we had been separated, I looked at her with disgust and thought of her as trash but I had to learn how to put my feelings aside for my kids. I knew that her return wouldn't be this hot and heavy rekindling—I wasn't delusional—but I did think we had a shot of going back to a new normal for the kids' sake if we worked on it. By this I mean, raising our children in a safe home and growing in the same direction, hopefully toward some sort of financial freedom.

But I was wrong. When Danielle moved in, she wouldn't let me touch her. I couldn't hug her. I couldn't kiss her or barely converse with her. When I mentioned this to her, there was always an excuse. It was clear that we didn't have a relationship of any kind. Rather, we were just roommates at that point and I suspected that she was still seeing the other guy and that was a difficult time for me because I worked overnight.

Winters in Philly can be brutal but that was the coldest year of my life.

I was struggling so badly financially and I didn't know what to do. Despite a half decent job. I had little to no money and was in debt. I noticed that my childhood friend and now Billionaire Michael Rubin, was doing well and had given a few of our other friends a little money from time to time to help them out. I gave him a ring, thinking this one phone call would be my saving grace. It took a lot of courage to make that call, you know, because pride is a large pill to swallow. It wasn't easy for me to ask for help so I did so indirectly.

On the phone, I said to Mike, "Hey man, I'm about five to seven grand in debt and could use some advice. Can you help me out?"

"Of course, of course," he said. "Meet me at the warehouse office on Wednesday."

I showed up to the KPR Sports warehouse with my bills and other financial documents, and Michael sat me down with his numbers guy. The accountant looked through my materials, and instructed me to come back in 20 minutes. When I popped my head in the office, he said, "I think you're going to be okay. If you get another part-time job, you can have this paid off within a year."

Mike had the biggest smile on his face knowing that he helped a friend just like I asked him to.

I was so crushed inside. I wanted him to just give me five to seven grand cash to pay off my debts. Instead, the accountant told me I had to find a part time job in addition to my full-time job.

I mustered up a "thank you guys," and on my way out, Mike said "Lenny, hold up." He went over to his closet, walked back towards me and handed me a small cardboard box.

"Don't open this until you get home brother."

Suddenly I was thrilled again. I thought this angel had just handed me a small box of cash that I desperately needed.

So, I rushed home, kicked off my shoes, and opened the box to find a set of Anthony Robbins motivational CDs.

I was disappointed, so I threw them in the trash.

Soon after I tossed those CDs, I decided that I could at least dig them out and listen to them on my forty-minute drive to work every night. What would it hurt?

That was, without a doubt, one of the greatest decisions I ever made in my life. It was the first time I learned how to consciously shift my mindset. I started thinking more about how the universe could help to bring success into my life instead of blindly chasing it. I learned how to create solid goals and then actively take steps to move forward to achieve them and pivot when necessary. I learned how to no longer be afraid of success and I learned how to embrace the power within myself. And, from there, I started listening to other motivational speakers—people like Jim Rohn, Zig Ziglar, Stephen Covey and Les Brown. I caught the bug. I needed to open my mind and expand my horizons so much more. To fully embrace my situation and start participating in life in a way that would open more doors and more opportunities. I can't thank my boy enough for giving me that box of motivational CDs. It was worth way more than cash and I will always love and respect him for being a good friend.

I weighed in at 270lbs, so I found this weight loss product called Herbalife. After using it for a while, it helped me to lose seventy pounds. I thought, hell, I could work with them to make a few extra bucks since my before-and-after photos are so stunning. I contacted the representative and he set me up. I would wear a button that said, "Lose Weight Now! Ask Me How!" And I wore another button that showed my before-and-after pictures. I had so many people come up and ask me how, so I'd get them set up on Herbalife, too.

I made about an extra $2,500 a month on top of my full-time job. So, Michael Rubin's accountant was right. I started paying down my debt and felt proud of myself.

Part of that MLM gig was to go to people's homes to try and sell them on the product. With every sale I closed, I made a commission. I was hustling and putting my new mindset to work. But Danielle wasn't having it. I'd tell her that I needed to go to a potential client's house, and she would start asking questions. And if it was ever a woman's home, I caught hell. She pulled me down instead of lifting me up and supporting me which, in turn, would support our family.

To make matters worse, she was still being cold to me.

So, after a year, I told her she needed to go back to her momma's house. I didn't want to just coexist. What's a marriage without touch? Without love? Without bonding or building?

She took the girls and moved back in with her mom and dad but I still watched them everyday after school.

I had a little whiteboard on the fridge for notes, and on that board, I wrote a date exactly one year from the day she moved out. I said that, if on that date, things haven't changed, I'll give up for good and just focus on being a single parent.

And for that year, I tried my hardest. I was kind. I was respectful. I caused no fights and no arguments. I was a good man, an honorable man. I invested so much time in trying to make her happy. It was a lonely time for me and it was embarrassing. I had very little pride and I am thankful my cousin Reggie Roberts was there to help me through some of it.

Around Christmas time, I took my kids over to see my mom at her home in Norristown. She asked me if I had finished my Christmas shopping yet and of course I hadn't. She offered to watch my 3 kids and I went to the King of Prussia Mall to buy that last item, a scooter for Jordan. Just as I was walking into Modell's Sporting Goods, I saw Danielle—my wife—holding hands with a completely different man. This time a black dude.

I approached her.

"Excuse me, can I please talk to you?" I asked.

"Who are you?" the guy asked.

"Her husband."

"She told me she was divorced," he said.

"We're not divorced. We're separated. Give us five minutes."

When I got Danielle to the side, I asked her what she was doing.

"You're walking in the mall, holding hands with another man. It's heartbreaking. Why can't you just wait until we're divorced?"

She looked me square in the eyes and said, "Fuck you."

So, I smiled and walked away. Throughout all the bullshit she put me through, I never felt more sad and hopeless. When she would spew this vitriol at me, I did not return it.

I simply walked away, into Modell's to buy our sweet child a scooter. And when I came out, I ran into my cousin and Nimmy's sister, Fee-Fee Tuggle who looked upset. She started crying saying that she saw Danielle holding hands with another dude.

"It's alright cuz, we've been separated for a while now."

Nevertheless, it was a humiliating moment!

The day concerning the whiteboard on the refrigerator finally came. Twelve months had gone by so quickly. I was nervous as hell. I opened the fridge, took a swig of orange juice, put it back, then picked up the phone.

"Hey, I just wanted to call and tell you that we should try to work it out. I truly believe this and I'm willing to try again. Today, I'd like to ask you to put aside everything. Let's work it out. I'm asking you for our family's sake to get back together and live in the same household. To raise our kids the right way, get them off to college and to a better life. Can we work it out?"

There was a long pause.

"No," she said. "I want a divorce."

I don't know what I was thinking. Honestly, I no longer wanted her back at this point so I guess I was just going through the motions.

So, I said, "Okay. Not a problem, I give up."

And within an hour, I was filing divorce papers downtown and would not look back. My family man identity was gone. I had three beautiful children, thank God, but life wasn't about to get easier. Losing a family, losing a marriage, it's devastating. I felt like it was the biggest failure of my life because I had tried so hard to get out of Norristown, to grow and to teach myself how to be a man, to be successful, and to be a damn-good father and husband. I wanted to break the chains of my family's failures. For a short while, I was proud that I established myself as a family man. I was happy that I was moving upward and forward in my life, and then it came tumbling down. I lost friends that I made over the years because I was so focused on making my family work, and then it fell apart anyway. I thought it was me who couldn't keep it together. In retrospect, I was a little too hard on myself.

To make matters worse, Danielle refused to sign the divorce papers for two whole years. It would be an ongoing battle for twenty-four months straight and I just wanted to get it over with so I could move on.

I didn't know it then but when Mom Mom and Pop Pop moved back down south to Georgia in the 90's to retire, it would be the eventual spark that I would rely on in the future. My little cousin Sean Tuggle and I moved in with them. He was in Middle School, and I was 20 with a job at a restaurant to help with the bills. We would hang-out with our older cousins Rick, Jimmy, Tony and Mike Coates. They all had their own houses and nice cars. My cousin Rick would come by my grandparents' house from time to time. He had a long driveway to his house and seemed like he had his shit together. He drove his car around and always had a scotch in hand. They all had money and it was great watching my cousins be successful. I was still trying to figure out life, so I took notice. After 8 months or so, I moved back up to Norristown. It was my twenty-first birthday when I caught that Greyhound bus.

Many years later, my Pop Pop passed away first and then Mom Mom. The family headed to Macon, Georgia for her funeral. I stayed with Rick and one night while we were chilling, I asked him how he managed to afford such a nice lifestyle.

Here is where that spark comes into play from all those years ago.

"Real estate," he said.

"Real estate?" I asked.

"Yeah, real estate."

"You think I'd be good at real estate?"

Without missing a beat, he said, "Yeah, I think you'd be alright at real estate. You got integrity?"

"Yeah."

"Give the best to your clients?"

"Yeah."

"Then you'd do alright."

And that particular conversation on that trip is one of the reasons I am where I am today. You see, Rick's younger brothers, Jimmy and Tony were the first to get involved in real estate. Rick saw what they were doing and then jumped in. He took it to a whole other level by becoming a broker and buying up foreclosures. Hell, even Mike, the youngest of them, had investment properties all over Macon, Georgia.

In 2002, I had a new dream, a new passion, and I was committed to learning everything I could about real estate.

Meanwhile, I still had divorce papers that needed to be signed by Danielle. I made several valiant attempts to get her to sign the papers—which is ironic given that she was the one who wanted the relationship to end, and she was the one who straight up asked for a divorce. I tried over and over and she kept putting it off until I told her that we were out of time. I let her know that I was going to stop by the bar where she worked because there was a deadline to sign the documents. She said okay and promised that she would sign the papers after she closed up. Here I was thinking that we'd hook up one last time, sign the papers, then part ways, only seeing each other when we needed to pick the girls up or drop them off.

So, she closed up and we walked out to the parking lot, papers in hand, when some guy rolled up on me yelling, "Yo! Yo! You ain't supposed to be near her. Get away from her."

I said, "Why am I not supposed to be near my wife? Who the fuck are you?"

"Fuck you, that's my girlfriend."

I had no clue that she was asking me to wait until she got off because her boyfriend Brian, was waiting at the other end of the bar. Dude was recklessly eyeballing me as she served me free drinks for a couple of hours. She could have signed the divorce papers when I got there and I would have left.

So, in the parking lot, he and his friend started walking toward me, so I turned and walked towards them, and she grabbed me by the back of my neck with her nails deep into my skin and yanked me to the ground. He jumped on top of me and tried to hit me, but I pushed him off me and got up and did what anyone from Norristown would do—I started fighting. His buddy jumped in, I punched the supposed boyfriend and broke his jaw, his buddy tackled me so I got up and punched him too. I jumped in my car, drove right to the police station and filed a police report.

I tried to press charges against all of them, but the Delaware County judge threw it out. He took one look at Brian who was white and then Danielle, who was mixed race but pretty much looked white, and he threw it the fuck out. Big shocker there!

At the next child support hearing for Danielle and I, a different Delaware County judge told us that I had to pay more in child support than I had already been paying. I realize that support payments do go up after a while but, it was a figure that was astronomical in comparison and neither of our salaries had increased and there was no occurrence that triggered an increase. Danielle later told me that her mother Marsha recommended that she get an increase in support so Danielle requested an increase from the court. I had experience with these hearings so I said, "Your Honor, I know how this works. I know there's a chart that you have, and you go down that chart. You look at what I make. You look at what she makes then you figure out who will cover health insurance plus daycare or school and that's what deter-mines how much I'd pay. Also, she lives with her parents and does not pay rent. Whereas, I have a mortgage. So the amount you just assigned me is excessive."

"You're telling me how to do my job?" the judge asked. "You're telling *me about my job*? Put him in cuffs."

Surprisingly, Danielle started shouting no and asked the judge to not arrest me. Gotta be honest, I thought I was going straight to jail.

"Mr. Bazemore, are you going to tell me how to do my job?"

"No, your Honor," I said. "But I do know how it works in Montgomery County because I have a child support case up there and I'm sure it works the same here in Delaware County. And the Judge over there invited my son's mother and I into her Chambers and showed us how the system works so we could agree on terms. I'm sorry if it's different here."

"Are you going to pay the additional child support or not?" he asked.

"Your Honor, I'm like most Americans, I live paycheck to paycheck and if I pay the excessive child support—which she's not entitled to—then I cannot pay my mortgage. I need a clean, safe home so that my kids can come visit me."

"Are you going to pay?"

"I can't pay that much more, your Honor."

The Judge with absolutely no honor said with an angry tone, "Then take him the hell away."

And just like that, the bailiff started taking me away. Danielle was screaming as I was still handcuffed and being escorted out.

"Mr. Bazemore, are you going to pay?" he asked one last time.

If I didn't pay, I would be thrown in jail, lose my job and I wouldn't be there for my beautiful kids. I wasn't about to be like JB or Hampton. I *wanted* to be in my kids' lives.

Defeated and pissed off, I said, "Yes, your Honor. I'll pay."

"Do you have any money now?"

"No, your Honor, but I'll pay when it's due."

And so, I paid the child support when it was due, and consequently, I couldn't pay my mortgage.

My house was eventually foreclosed on, and all that money that I put into it went down the drain. After all that work, after all that energy, time, and a desire to build a safe haven for my kids, it was gone and now I had bad credit too.

Thankfully, my girlfriend Mimi let me move in with her. We

were seeing each other so much that we decided living together and splitting the bills fifty-fifty would make the most sense. After my life had settled a bit, I remembered my cousins down in Georgia and decided to pursue real estate and so for the next four months, I studied at Polley Associates School of Real Estate in Pa.

My childhood friend Craig Salamone told me that once I got my license, I could work at his father's agency, Salamone Realty in Plymouth Meeting, Pa.

The night before I took the test that would grant me a real estate license in Pennsylvania, I partied too hard. I felt reckless and self-destructive as I failed the exam. But that prince from Norristown, he was still deep inside of me, dreaming of something more. And so, I took the test a second time. And a third, then a fourth. And suddenly, I became worried about that so-called prince inside of me, but his winning mentality was so strong that he searched deep down and remembered that he played on 7 championship winning sports teams in the past. He was a fucking winner and the music in his head sounded an awful lot like Freddie Mercury belting, "We are the champions, my friends. And, we'll keep on fighting 'till the end."

I decided that when I scheduled the fifth test, it would be my last.

Working at night and going to real estate school in the morning was an efficient way to get ahead in life. I benefited from using my time wisely. At this point, I was working at Glen Mills for 10 years before Mike Schneider came along. Mike was brought on to be the new supervisor of the third shift after not cutting it on the second shift. The night shift, that was a different breed of human. We were nocturnal. We were family. Most of us had been with the company for years, working the same schedule and none of us liked Mike. He was a self conscious, shallow fucking asshole with very little integrity. He wanted everyone to like him and kiss his ass to make himself feel important.

After each shift, we'd have a team meeting in which we'd discuss the things that went well and the things that did not go well. One morning, during a team meeting, I took the last sip out of my water bottle and casually placed it in the trash can that was right next to me. Something about that pissed Mike off because he looked at me and shouted, "Excuse me!"

And you know, my smart ass quipped back, thinking his reaction was more than over the top, "You're excused Mike!" Which makes everyone snicker.

"Meeting ADJOURNED!" He shouted.

Us normal people walked out of the building laughing up a storm while we headed to our cars in the back parking lot when suddenly, Mike sped up behind us, window down.

"Lenny, get in the car."

Trying to be funny, I said "Excuse me?"

"Can you please get in the car?"

I said "yeah" and got in his car.

"What's your problem with me?" he asked.

"I don't have a problem with you, Mike."

"Well, I don't understand what the disrespect is about then."

"What disrespect Mike? You feel like I'm disrespecting you?"

This sent him into a tizzy. He started stuttering as if I told him I was going to burn his mother's house down. Dude was deeply shallow and insecure. More specifically, he was rude and he wasn't a true third shifter like us.

"Man, I'm just doing my job," I said. "I do my job as good as anybody else. I don't come here to kiss anyone's ass, though. Are you asking me to kiss your ass Mike?"

"Just get out of my car and have a good weekend."

And so, I got out of his car, walked over to mine, and drove home. I had 3 days off and would return to work on Tuesday night at 11:00pm.

Working that night shift job was extremely hard on my body but it was also an advantage. It allowed me to take real estate practice tests throughout the early morning and each one was a success.

I tried to get off work early that next Saturday morning so I could take the 5th real estate exam but Mike was being an asshole as usual. He would not let me leave 30 minutes sooner to take a test that could change my life. All good because it just made me more determined and so after work, I hauled ass to the testing center, missing my opportunity by just ten minutes. All the test spots were filled.

"I'm sorry," the woman behind the counter said. "No more tests today."

I was pissed the fuck off and walked out.

But In that moment, God would not allow any weapons formed against me to prosper!

The woman came running out of the front door as I was getting in my car.

"Sir," she yelled and waved. "We have one spot left."

Someone just said they were too nervous to take the exam so you can have their time slot.

Walking into that room knowing I was going to pass my real estate exam was a triumphant feeling. I seized on an opportunity that was now completely under my control and there was nothing that was going to stand in my way.

I knew as soon as I sat in front of that computer, I would ace it. I passed with flying colors and it was time to enter a new world of making money.

People think real estate is an easy gig. Study a little bit, take and pass the exam, pay a few hundred for your license, then suddenly you rake in six-figures on a slow day.

That's Bullshit!

You must study your ass off for months and months, pass a very difficult multi-part exam, do research to find reputable companies to interview and then choose and sign with the right broker. Then, you must apply the knowledge, find a good mentor, pave your own way, pay attention to contracts and real estate law, then hustle every waking hour you possibly can. You are an independent contractor basically working for yourself and you must have discipline. There is no such thing as a part-time Realtor. It's full-time only. You see, when you're a young father with a couple of college credits, with no one else to rely on for basic needs, you find a way to make the impossible possible. The reality shows on TV make it seem easy. They sensationalize it but it's one of the hardest commission-based industries to crack because if you don't sell, then you don't eat.

I would see my 3 kids every other weekend at this stage in life. During the weekdays, I worked a full-time job in the real estate office learning what I could. Then, I'd go home to get 4-5 hours of sleep then go to my other full-time night job as a security guard for the infamous Glen Mill Schools—a reform school that was founded in 1826 for boys between the ages of twelve and twenty-one that was closed in 2019 because of misconduct and abuse. That was the only job that actually paid since I wasn't selling any houses just yet. I had been working for Glen Mills for ten years and my responsibilities were to secure the campus and to make sure the students didn't run away in the middle of the night. We'd check on them periodically, usually around every fifteen minutes. We'd check on the staff housing across the street, the golf course, you know, the entire estate. Basically, we'd take care of anything that needed to be handled all night long. Every now and then, I was asked to run the switchboard, which reminded me of my mother and her days at Bell Telephone.

One night, I was working as the campus rover checking to make sure all campus buildings were locked and secure. It started to rain and I was rushing back to the van when I slipped and fell down a hill injuring my back. I went through the whole ordeal of workplace injury—workman's compensation, physical therapy and all. As a result of falling, my back would occasionally lock up and one night, I just couldn't get out of bed. Like, physically unable to. So, I called in sick. You know, because I'm a courteous person and I value my employment, (which really means I needed the fuckin' job!)

Mike called the switchboard operator and told him to document that I did not call in sick and I did not show up. The switchboard operator who was working that night was named Carlin. He called me to tell me what Mike did but I was fired from the Glen Mills Schools that morning!

Over my 10 year period of employment, I was never written up or given any type of discipline or warning for an incident. I was never in any altercations or had problems with another employee or student on or off campus. I rarely called in sick and I came in and did my job better than others. I was the youngest team leader on the squad and well liked throughout the school and it was a good gig while it lasted. Everyone started having issues when bitch ass Mike came on board. I always wanted to say to management, "Fuck you and thank you for firing me." Life is crazy like that. When one door closes another may open. So, I read the book "Who moved my cheese" and then decided that if I was going to make this real estate dream work, I should focus on it alone and I never looked back.

It was 2003, three years after Danielle and I separated, and she still hadn't signed the divorce papers. So naturally, that started to cause some tension with my girlfriend Mimi, who was asking me to get married and have a kid with her. That might have been flattering to someone else, but for me—a man with three little ones, no thanks! I was already struggling to provide for my kids so that was off the table. And I was very clear about it. I told her to let me officially get divorced, save some money and together we'd then figure out a plan. Pretty reasonable, right?

I don't know what was going through her mind, but it was not cool because she began following me when I would go out with the fellas. She provided detailed accounts of my outings, too. I would come home to her telling me where I had gone and who I was with and all that bullshit, I realized I had to get out of her place. So, one day when she was at work, I packed up all my shit and asked my boy Craig if I could stay at his place or at least keep some of my shit in his finished basement. Like a good friend, he said I could move in if I paid $600 a month in rent. Some of his mortgage would get paid and I'd have a place to stay. When I got there, I called her and told her that it was over, that I left some money on the counter, but I was done.

Mimi showed up at Craig's house once, looking frail after losing an unhealthy amount of weight. She acknowledged how crazy she had acted, we parted ways amicably, and I wished her well and haven't heard from her since.

I was excited when I signed with Salamone Realty of Plymouth Meeting, PA. because I knew them since I was a kid. The first year of having my license, I didn't sell one house until my eleventh month. Probably because I put such a heavy emphasis on learning everything I possibly could about the industry. To get good, you gotta learn how to be good and to do that, you have to know the information inside and out. In my second year, things changed. Remember, I was fired from my full-time night job and real estate is all I had. I became the number-one salesperson in the office. I give the Salamones some credit for that. Like I said, I grew up with Jeff and his brother Craig, so they were like family to me. Jeff and his father Nick were instrumental in teaching me the keys to success in real estate early on. Jeff taught me literally everything he knew, and I read all the books I could get my hands on—you know, back in those beginning of the internet days.

We had these thick books with the addresses of every house on and off the market since there was no online system for real estate yet. Nowadays, you can just pull out your phone, log onto the MLS (multiple listing service,) pull up the address, and go off to sell or list a property and use electronic signatures. It was a tough process back then. Every day we'd get new listings in the book. And if you wanted to show a property, you literally had to go to the book, pull the page out, make a copy at the Xerox machine, then put it back for the next person. So inefficient, but it was all we had. At the end of the day though, I busted my ass and became very good at real estate.

Overall, my time with the Salamones' was amazing. It was one of those magical times in a person's life where your friends feel like real family because you're working so intimately with them and I attended most of their family functions. Jeff and I worked so well together. We thought we were going to take over his family business and run it together one day. We were completely emotionally invested. I remember times when Jeff would come over to Craig's early in the morning, down into the basement where I stayed, and he'd wake me up by pouring a cup of cold water on me. Naturally I'd scramble out of bed, yelling, "What the fuck dude!" And he always replied, "Early bird! Early bird gets the worm!" Jeff is a good dude. He'd wait for me to get showered and dressed, then we'd hit the Dunkin' Donuts, and then head into the office. I knew that he was proud of me and he cared about my success. Those years provided me with a lot of value, mostly because they allowed me to really come into my own as a real estate professional, a moment to really grow my expertise in the business. I built up a lot of confidence and coupled with a little business knowledge —I was preparing to be unstoppable.

Things were going well for everyone, and time was flying by. Craig was still working for Michal Rubin's company and had been since he was 18 or so. I don't think he has ever worked for anyone else in his entire life. On some nights we would hit up the local bars and everywhere we went, we were the cool-kids. I was hanging with my friends Shawn Burns, Braheen Mitchell and Malcolm Poindexter III. We were good looking, charismatic men who always became the life of the party. I was careful with the little money I had because I had 3 kids to care for and Craig always seemed to pay for everyone anyway. On some weekends, we would head down to the Jersey Shore in Atlantic City and stay in huge suites at the Borgata Casino that just opened. There were times when professional athletes like retired Philadelphia Eagles, Mike Quick and Seth Joyner would show up and hang out with us. Rubin would also rent mansions in Miami Beach for a month at a time for all his friends. Any one of us could go down and stay for as long as we wanted but we had to get there on our own. One day a few Playboy models showed up and we had this crazy day party. I was sitting by the pool when I received a phone call from my attorney letting me know that my divorce was finalized. I celebrated by ordering "Domino's Pizza" and going to my room alone with a bottle of Patron Silver. I ate and sipped in peace. A Spanish model came looking for me so I gave her a slice of pizza and told her I needed privacy. I also told her that I would catch up with her at the club later. The time came to get dressed for the night and head to Club Privé at Opium Miami for bottle service. We would then head back to the mansion for a wild party. While standing at the front door of the Mansion before we left, I looked over at my friend James "Gucci" Morrissey and said "Can you believe this is our life?" and he said, "Absolutely."

Back home in Pa., we would go to dinner at high end restaurants like Buddakan then hit up Club Denim in downtown Philly. It was an insane time and Craig Salamone was the glue of it all, but Michael Rubin was the real saint behind the scenes. Both of them always made sure their boys tasted some of the good life. As Rubin's childhood friend, I would like the entire world to know that he is the real deal. People naturally gravitate towards him because of his brilliance and he has always been compassionate towards other peoples, race, religion and culture. Honestly, he is one of the most authentic guys you will ever meet. He is a very nice person and super intelligent, caring, generous and empathetic and I hope he runs for President of the United States one day. I would absolutely vote for him, and I think he would win and heal this country.

During this time period in the early 2000's, I figured out that it would be good to have multiple revenue streams of income coming in so, in addition to real estate, I started my first e-commerce business. A T-shirt brand and mission that focused on erasing racism, promoting one love and bringing people of all races together to share a common respect for each other. I made a lot of money but was never highly successful with it.

Life has a funny way of making things interesting when you get too comfortable in a situation. Life started to get a little tense around the Salamones.' There was an incident at Craig's house that was the beginning of the end. We used to go to the Valley Tavern, a local bar to drink and sing karaoke and then invite a bunch of people back to his crib to continue the party. Sometimes we knew them and sometimes it was random people. One night, I thought a few of the people that came back to the house were shady as fuck. I told Craig about my intuition and said we should ask them to leave, but he shrugged it off because he liked to show people a good time. The next morning when he realized his Rolex Yacht-Master was stolen, I had a hunch who did it. I thought the shady tall white dude was to blame and told him to immediately call the cops, get a police report and then call his insurance company. He never did either one! A few days went by, then he started acting weird and insinuating that maybe I knew where it was. Basically, that's the same as telling me that I stole it and that pissed me the fuck off. Why in the world would I do something so fucked up to a friend that I was loyal to and risk losing my shelter? A place where my kids came to visit me. That was my home at the time, and you don't shit where you eat! I had his back, and he couldn't care less about my loyalty. You see, when my ex-wife ruined our marriage and my life came crashing down a couple of years prior, I didn't know what to do. I had nowhere to turn. He was there for me that day when I could not hold in the pain any longer. He let me cry on his shoulder so, the best way for me to repay him for that, was to have his back no matter what! I respected and loved my friend but, I felt the shift happening and after two years of living with him, I completely realized that I overstayed my welcome.

His father Nick, for whatever reason and I'm sure it was unrelated, withheld my real estate commission from a house that I sold. Also, he and I would argue about the 50-50 commission split because after 2 years, I thought I deserved more like 70-30 or at a minimum 60-40 since I did all of my own deals and settlements with very little help from the office. Unfortunately, it seemed like my time at Salamone Realty was up too, so I put in my notice and went to work with Goldfarb & Davis Realty (G&D) down in Philadelphia.

I still lived with Craig and the end of the month was coming up so rent was due. Craig and another friend of ours named Carlton Smith, literally just received $15,000 each from Michael Rubin from a quick trip to Atlantic City, NJ and then again a couple of weeks later in Las Vegas making it $30K a piece. I paid my child support for the month and a few other bills, leaving me just $200 short for rent. Of course, I wouldn't have been short if Craig's father had paid my commission on time. And how does Craig roll up into his house the next day trying to impress his stripper girlfriend? With several Neiman Marcus bags, acting like a bigshot baller after telling me I better have his $200 bucks. He may have been charismatic with a great smile, but narcissism is easy to spot.

So, I said to him, "Must be nice."

"Fuck you," he said. "You BETTER have my money tomorrow?"

I went downstairs to his basement, hoping to figure out how to make another $200 bucks real quick so I could pay him the remaining rent. I always felt like his girlfriend was trying to get me and his other friends out of the picture. At exactly midnight, he opened the door to the basement and asked if I had his money. When I said no, he started poppin' off, yelling something about, "You better get my fucking money you lazy motherfucker" and I snapped.

This man was hounding me over $200 when our mutual friend just gave him thousands just because.

For years I had focused on becoming the best version of myself that I could possibly be. I had suppressed that poor kid from Norristown and replaced him with the family man, Leonard Arnett Bazemore, husband and father of three. I left my hometown and built a life outside of it where no one knew what I was doing or what I was going through and at that point in my life, I didn't have a lot of money but I was successful because I was still alive.

And that night in Craig's house, the old Lenny from the streets of Norristown came back—full force.

I ran up the stairs, grabbed him by the shirt and put him against the wall. I called him a motherfucker, and said, "Did you forget who you are talking to? I'm Lenny fucking Bazemore and I'll beat your punk ass."

I was always the man when we were growing up. And he was always the guy watching me be the man. As a matter of fact, everyone I grew up with knew I was the man back in the day. The handsome dude that the girls chased. The popular guy who had multicultural friends from all the surrounding communities. The cool dude at every party. The chill brotha that other guys wanted to be. The sports star who was on his way to the big leagues. They weren't the ones who were signing autographs after high school football games. I was! And I was seconds away from pulverizing him, but I chose not to.

At that moment, he kicked me out of his home and I lost my shelter. I had already lost my family and now a possible friendship too. So, I packed up some of my shit and I left.

It was the middle of the night and I had nowhere to go. I was homeless.

TEN

Lucky to be Alive

No money in my pocket but thankful I had gas in the tank. With half of my shit in the car, I drove down to the Valley Tavern—the place where all are welcomed, no matter where you come from. I asked the bartender for a much-needed beer but told her I didn't have any money.

"It's no problem, baby," she said and poured me one.

I started crying. What a grand gesture for someone who was in such need.

So there I was, at the bar, looking straight out of a country song. Tears in my beer, racking my brain tryin' to figure out what I was gonna do. Thinkin', thinkin', thinkin' but I had no clue. Had nowhere to go and I had no dough. Sleeping in my car was the only option at 12:30 am. Eventually I was going to have to pay child support. I had so much to consider, which made the tears flow even harder.

Literally, like an angel, this young blonde woman came out of nowhere, put her hand on my back, and said, "Why are you crying? Are you okay?"

"No, I'm not okay," I said. "I just got kicked out of my friend's house for being $200 late with rent when our mutual friend recently gave him $30 grand just because. His father owes me $1,500 in real estate commissions. I have nowhere to go. I have three kids. No money. Nowhere to sleep. I just don't know what I'm gonna to do."

"Stop crying," she said. "You can stay with me tonight."

I had never met this woman in my life. But she told me to follow her, so I did. I followed her a few blocks down the road, then she said she needed to talk to her roommate before she allowed me in since her roommate had a little kid.

After what felt like eternity, but I'm sure it was only a minute, the kind woman came back and said it was fine if I slept on the couch.

"You'll be safe tonight."

And so, I slept there.

The next morning, I woke up, folded the blanket, and I left a thank you note.

I found enough change in my car to go to the 7-Eleven and buy a cup of coffee, and the dude behind the counter gave me his newspaper. With the last of my money tied up with Salamone Realty and no place to go, I figured I'd better start looking for a short-term solution. I turned to the classifieds and immediately saw a help wanted ad for a live in handyman. It was about eight in the morning, and I gave the number a ring. When someone picked up, I said I was calling about the ad in the paper and the woman on the other end, an old lady who liked to be called Aunt May, in what sounded like an impression of a grown ass Minnie Mouse, told me to come down and talk about it.

When I got there, her nurse had to come unlock the security gate on the porch and let me in. It was a big four-story brick home in Powelton Village, West Philly and was a little dirty. You know, she was an old woman in an old house, but as soon as I saw Aunt May sitting in her big chair—this adorable light-skinned, chubby cheeked lady with pufferfish lips—I knew we were kindred spirits.

"How are you doing?" she asked.

"I'm great, how are you today?"

"I'm fine, what's your name?"

"My name is Lenny Bazemore and what can I help you with?"

She told me what she needed, all common and minor home repairs and totally manageable.

And then she goes, "Do you wanna know how I got this house?"

"Yes, how'd you get this house?"

"I was a gambler. I played poker. I paid for this house by winning in poker."

Man, that shit was hilarious!

"You know, I can help you if you want. It's no problem." I said.

"Okay, when can you move in?" she asked.

I said, "Today, I can move in today!" But that's how my life works sometimes, you know? One door closes, another opens. That's how prayer and taking action works. That's how God works.

The nurse unlocked the door to my new bedroom. You see, when you live in a room in a house where other people live too, you have to put the padlock on the door every time you leave or your shit might go missing. We opened the door to the room and the entire place was painted blue. And I mean, everything, every part of it was blue. And the condition of the room was poor. Nasty. Trash everywhere. Bugs, dirt, pure filth! I spent all day cleaning it out. I reached out to Craig and asked him if I could come get the last of my stuff. I had to make two trips, and on the last run, I put a few crates of CDs and DVDs on the top of the rear trunk of my car because I was not in the right frame of mind and didn't mean to.

I drove off for good, leaving behind two years of memories both good and bad. I headed to Aunt May's house and when I made a turn, I noticed something fly off the back of my car.

I was on Germantown Pike, A busy main street with two lanes in each direction. There were no passing cars, which was extremely odd, so I pulled into someone's driveway to go get my belongings.

Of course, I was in emotional distress. I had just gone separate ways with Craig, a dear friend since we were kids. I was in the process of moving out and laying my head down in a strange new place. It was dark and late, and I kept thinking about the catchphrase that Jeff Salamone and I used to say when times were challenging. "Everything's going to be alright, but nothing's going to be ok." I wasn't in the right frame of mind at that moment.

I was in the street, on my hands and knees, picking up the CDs and DVDs when I heard a loud horn blaring! Suddenly, I looked up to see a car barreling towards me, headlights blinding me, brakes screeching, and I could smell the hot metal as the car passed by. Literally, just a few inches away from my head.

I was in shock. It was so dark out. I jumped up! I backed up a few steps right into on-coming traffic just as another car came barreling at me, screeching their breaks too. As a reaction, I stretched out my hands to stop the car, but it hit me and knocked me back and onto the ground.

I've never felt luckier to be alive.

Just for fun, let's do some counting.

A shard of glass thrown at my head when I was 4. Almost bled to death. Lucky to be alive.

Stabbed twice. Lucky to be alive. Hell, lucky to be walking.

A gun pointed to my head. Lucky to be alive.

Almost killed by two cars. Lucky to be alive.

When I tell you that my dad wore a condom and that I've been fighting since day one to be alive, I fucking mean that shit.

The woman in the second car got out and asked if I was okay, but I wasn't. I was basically mentally numb at that point. My neck hurt, my elbows and upper back felt like they were on fire. My lower back was throbbing and my pride was shattered. I put my shit in the car and went to the spot where my sister Tara was bartending at the time. She gave me a shot and a beer, but I couldn't stop shaking. Eventually, I went back to Aunt May's, and I cried my eyes out all night long in my new home. It was there that I started to rebuild my life step by step. And this time, the story wasn't going to end with me being homeless, penniless, broken or depressed, none of that shit! This time, I was going to fucking make it. And I promised myself that no matter what, I was unstoppable and one day, I would be sitting in that house on the hill, holding hands with a beautiful, educated wife, with my kids by my side and I would never have to worry about money again.

It took a minute, but I learned how to forgive Craig even though he spoke bad about me to some mutual friends. (of course, it all got back to me but none of the things he said were true because I. Am. Not. a piece of shit!)

Yes, he can be a fucking ass sometimes, but what's strange is that he is a walking contradiction because he also has one of the biggest hearts you will ever find in a person. I believe that he has created an isolated lifestyle to protect himself from the outside world and will never fully have the quality of life he truly desires. I pray he finds healing, peace and true happiness one day. I believe therapy can work for anyone.

On that night, he should have treated me with the respect that I deserved. However, he was there for me when I needed him the most, and I still care about him for that. Also, I still care about his entire family.

20 years ago, I know I stayed at his place way too long trying to get myself together and that's on me and me alone. If he ever needs advice, all he has to do is call because we grew up together. I still consider him a friend because we were able to talk it out a few years later. We're just not as close as we used to be.

ELEVEN

Thank God for Aunt May

Aunt May was one of the most important figures in my life before she passed away. Finding her was like finding another angel and I loved her very much. She became family and it was a win-win for the both of us. She needed a man around the house, friendship and assistance, while I benefited from the inexpensive housing and a place to restart my life. Her main needs included help getting up the stairs in her electric chair and then to her wheelchair, help getting into bed and help with bathing once in a while. It was a compassionate gig, and she was a tough lady that did not take a bit of shit from anyone.

When I left Salamone Realty, I was really hoping it would be the change I needed. I thought Goldfarb & Davis Realty would provide me with the stability to grow into my own and start making a serious name for myself as a 3rd year real estate agent. But as shit goes—at least in my life, anyway—the foundation started to shift again, and it began threatening the stability of my life. You see, after a while at G&D, I found out that the owner of the company wasn't a broker at all. If I recall correctly, the principal broker was someone else who lived and worked out in Chester County or some shit like that and they never came to the office. And if you know anything about real estate, you know that working with someone who isn't a legal broker can jeopardize your license and career. And I only found this out after I had to beg for my commissions because I didn't receive them for three or four weeks. I have done real estate deals where I got paid that day. The average turnaround back then was three business days after the deal closes. And when you got kids and bills to pay—three or four weeks doesn't fucking work. This was happening way too often. But hell, I was still crushing the real estate game because all of my clients were investors and kept me busy. I would find them off market deals. They would buy it and I would receive a commission. Then, they would renovate it and give me back the listing. I would receive another commission after it was sold. I loved making a commission on both ends.

I was making good money and felt great about myself—better than I did in a while, which is saying something since battling many years of depression. It was now time to get back in the gym. I found a spot called Bally Total Fitness in Center City, Philly on 15th and Walnut Streets. The energy in that gym was amazing and I decided that it was time to start working out again to balance my emotional, spiritual and physical levels. When I walked in, the general manager Michael Spishock came up to me right away and asked, "Are you here for the job?"

"Nah, I'm just here to work out."

"Oh, you look the part," he said. "Can I interview you?"

Now, how often does that happen? I mean really, you can't make this shit up.

"I just want a gym membership man," and somehow, I ended up in his office.

Within 20 minutes, I was hired. I didn't even say if I wanted the job or not and he was telling me I was hired. So I said okay, fine. I asked him to tell me what they paid, what the hours were like, all that good stuff.

"We'll give you a salary for the first three months, and you get commission for every sale you make. If you sell personal training, you get commission on that too. And if you do the personal training yourself, you get paid for that too. We'll certify you as a personal trainer, so don't worry about that." As an employee, I could work out for free as well.

"What?" I asked, completely astonished. "Where do I sign?"

All I wanted was to tone up and keep in shape but instead, I got a job as an assistant manager with a salary plus commissions times three. I was gettin' *paid* and working with some of the coolest dudes I've ever met. Guys like Brian Mendenhall, Mike Freeman and John Nester. Some other cool dudes who were around included Blake Warren and Jason Phillips.

Back at G&D, they were still fucking with my commission check. I was tired of asking and I shouldn't have to beg for what I've earned. I confronted the owner in the middle of the office with a raised voice and asked him, "Where the fuck is my money?" Only to be met with a wimpy, "Don't curse in this office."

"Let me tell you something dude! You better have my *fucking* money tomorrow." (side note…As I wrote this, it reminded me of Craig Salamone. lol)

And on my way out, I heard the ladies in the office whisper something about, "I can't believe he yelled at him." Let's just say, I had my money the next day!

Here's a life lesson for you: "Don't take shit from anybody but always try to be nice about it and never raise your voice and get angry. If someone owes you money, try to collect your money and if they don't pay then put a lien on their assets or just consider it a buyout and leave that relationship. The only thing that matters in this world is your peace of mind and taking care of your family. If you aren't always looking out for your best interest, then you'll never truly be happy in life." I don't recall where I got his from, but I always said, "If you don't look out for number one then you just might step in number two."

I was walking through the park in Rittenhouse Square enjoying a cup of coffee one morning when I just happened to run into Mr. Davis himself, co-founder of the real estate company

G&D and the one who signed me on to work there. I asked him what was going on at the office.

"You know, Pennsylvania Real Estate Commission law says I'm required to have my commission checks in three business days or less. What's the deal?"

There was a pause and then he goes, "Yeah... I left the company."

"Why?" I asked.

"Well, you know, I had to leave. I saw how things were starting to go over there with the broker situation and it's not good."

"Well, that's not cool. You should have at least given us a heads up. I don't fuck around with my real estate license. I worked too hard to get it and it's far too important of an asset in my goal to become financially independent."

That week, G&D was being bought out by Long and Foster. They were located in The Curtis Atrium building in Washington Square, Philly. This was obviously a legitimate real estate company. All of the agents went down for a meeting at their new office and listened to their spiel because they wanted to retain each of us. I told them what I thought of the office leadership and that, although I wanted to stay, it felt like a good time to take a break since I was doing well at Bally's and getting a steady paycheck.

And so, I put my real estate license in escrow. (For anyone who is not familiar with the term, that basically means that I put it in safekeeping to use at a later date; I wouldn't be able to perform as a real estate professional while it was in escrow, but when I did want to practice again, all I would have to do is answer a questionnaire from the PA Real Estate Commission then pay the fee to get it back to active status and then I could help people buy and sell their real estate assets again.)

I had my bills down to a minimum and was making 3-4 grand a month just through Bally's. I considered that to be crushing it back then. Not to mention, I made a lot of new friends. I was hanging out in Rittenhouse Square everyday, which is the most popular upscale neighborhood in Philly. It has all sorts of high-end restaurants, shops, people out and about, artists doing their crafts in the park and people hustling for a dollar.

With all the new socializing, I didn't have much time left for Aunt May, so we made a deal. Instead of being her handyman and helping her at night, she said I could just pay her $250 a month for rent which helped us both.

I had visitation with my 3 kids every other weekend, so when they'd come stay with me at Aunt May's, we'd go down to the supermarket, get some food or head over to the movie theater, maybe walk around the Drexel or the UPenn campus, go to the Zoo, hang out at Penn's Landing, catch the train downtown or just watch movies at home. We always had something to do. Time with Daddio was always magical. My son Devon went with the flow. My daughter Jordan got herself ready but Alexis was still little and complained sometimes when I did her hair. I think I did a great job because she always looked beautiful. She said I was a little too rough with her head. As a single father, I did the best I could but I think she was right.

And then Bally's changed the commission structure.

I went from making good money to basically making very little. They later filed for bankruptcy.

Times got tough again. Money constricted.

I would walk home from work instead of taking the $2 train. At certain times, I had to knock on the back of restaurants and ask if they had any extra food in exchange for a dollar. When coworkers would go to lunch, I wouldn't join them, but sometimes, if the hunger was powerful enough, I'd ask them to bring me back a sandwich and not really pay them back for it. If there was food left in the break room refrigerator, I'd pull the classic move, "You ain't gonna eat that, are you?" Some of them probably knew I had food insecurity.

I got real skinny during this time. So skinny that my abs started showing. My cheekbones were perky, my body was ripped, and this Jamaican girl I was seeing at the time always said that I looked like a model. But the fact of the matter is, I was starving. Sometimes at night, I would have to fight off the tears because I could not afford to cry myself to sleep. I thought I would become more hungry if I exerted the extra energy.

It got to the point where I was so hungry one night that I went downstairs to the dirty ass kitchen and found Aunt May's open can of salmon in the refrigerator that had roaches crawling near it. It was disgusting. And for a second, I almost ate it. That's how desperate times were, and I needed a new job, so I left Bally's for the Philadelphia Sports Clubs (PSC), which was more of a corporate gym. I was there maybe a year, and the allure of real estate was getting strong again, but I was stuck. Not to mention, my job at PSC was paying my bills and putting food in me and my kids' bellies. I didn't have the time to focus on real estate anyways. It was the quintessential catch 22.

In 2006, there was always time for socializing and having a little fun, even with very little money. And you know, Rittenhouse Square, that was a great place to be if you're trying to move up in the world. Point being, I got to know these two dudes, Tommy Dellapenna and Perry Milo—two artists who previously owned galleries in Philly. We became friends and I always had fun watching them paint in the Square.

Two other guys I became friends with were Elijah and Benjamin. Young professional dudes with college degrees. We'd go to happy hour where they'd spend money left and right. You know, young guys without families who were living a carefree life. And I was a cool guy with a storied background, a brilliant mind, and a passion to not just be successful, but to be financially independent. And those were the types of people I wanted to be around.

Elijah and Ben worked for an international commercial real estate company called Jones, Lang, LaSalle (JLL). And every time we'd go out to happy hour, they'd wear their suits and ties, coming straight from work. I would casually dress in jeans and a shirt. I must have impressed them and they must have valued my wisdom because one day they came to happy hour telling me how much they enjoyed hanging out with me.

Ben said, "You know, you should consider coming to work with us at JLL."

You can probably tell by now that falling into new opportunities is one of my superpowers. Doors opened for me because I learned how to manifest it.

"I'd love to," I said. Because I hated working at the corporate gym.

The guys were able to get me an interview. I put on one of my best suits that I got from Marshalls with a tax refund check back in 2002 when I first started working in real estate, and I went to the interview, confident as hell.

And guess what.

I nailed the fucking interview.

So much so, that the manager's exact words to me at the end were, "Oh my God, you are fucking phenomenal!"

To which I replied, "Thank you. Can I have the job?"

I had this dream one night of selling real estate in Spain.

"Well," he said, "listen, you nailed the interview. I think you are great. I've never met anyone like you. And I'm sure you'd do well at this job. I *want* to hire you. But I just can't because you don't have a college degree and that is a requirement."

I was stumped but I wasn't beat yet!

So I said, "Okay, fine. I'll tell you what, JLL has the employee tuition reimbursement program, right? If you hire me, I will then be able to afford school and promise, I'll enroll in college right away and I will get my degree at night by way of using your company reimbursement program."

"Wow!" he said. "You're amazing, but I just can't do it."

"Come on, take a chance on me. If I don't enroll in school, let's say within 30 days, then you can fire me. Straight up, I really need this job. I'm a single father with three kids. I was born and raised in Norristown and this job will make a huge difference in our lives. I will become the best salesperson you ever had."

"I have no doubt about that. But you don't have a degree."

I said, "When I was waiting in the lobby, I noticed the trophy case."

"Yeah," he said. "We play a competitive softball tournament every year. It's our office against other offices, and we were able to win a couple of the tournaments."

"Well, I'm a pretty good athlete. If you hire me, not only will I go to college immediately, but I will also ensure that you win every year. You'll have a new trophy in the case every year."

"Oh, my fucking God, dude! You're phenomenal. I promise you this. Go get a degree and I will hire you. I guarantee! I promise you that. Just go get a degree."

"Okay. Thank you for the interview."

We shook hands and I said I'd see him one day in the future.

"I hope so, Lenny. I really hope so."

Walking out of that office building, I felt both inspired and dejected. I mean, incredible disappointment. Had I gotten the job, I would have made over a hundred and twenty five grand my first year. That would have changed my entire life. I was saddened but I was also encouraged.

By that point in my life, I had experienced so much pain and suffering that I didn't stew in heartbreak and disappointment for too long. You see, I learned to embrace my feelings, I validate them, go through the process of feeling each of their emotions and then I think about my kids future and use that as inspiration to move on. That's how I became a solution based thinker.

I immediately enrolled in DeVry University, studying business courses at night. I already had about fifteen college credits. I never again wanted to be turned down from an opportunity because I didn't have a piece of paper that said I could complete academic work. You see, I was not entirely qualified for that role but I'm a fast learner and I would have done well. The guy interviewing me even thought so. I spent some time thinking about my experience in that interview and decided that I would conform and play by the socially constructed rules and get that piece of paper—and learn a few more things along the way.

In the meantime, I was still at the corporate gym. Dwayne "The Rock" Johnson came in to workout once. He was nice to everyone and took the time to take photos with all of the employees. It was cool meeting him and I also had a chance to help Barbara Streisand once. Her team said that she sometimes traveled with her treadmill and it wasn't working. I had our rep visit her hotel to fix it. As a thank you, they gave me two tickets to see her perform in Philly. I remember seeing Rosie O'Donnell sitting in the front row, happy as can be, jamming and singing every song. One of the perks of being employed there was working out for free. Most times after I finished for the day, I'd go home, get changed, hop on my bike for cardio and ride back to the gym to workout. One night while exercising after work, a member of the housekeeping staff approached me saying "there was someone looking for a gym membership."

"Uh, I'm busy working out," I told him.

The guy was persistent and said, "She seems like a nice lady," so I caved because I like nice ladies.

While I showed Teresa around the gym, she told me that she was new in town because she had recently taken a job as General Counsel (GC) of her company. I got on that one machine that tightens up the glutes, you know the one where you push back your leg and it tightens up your butt, and I said, "I'm gonna show you this machine, but don't look at my butt."

And I mean, of course she looked at my butt, so we started laughing. There was something special about her and the way she laughed. We immediately felt like friends. I showed her the rest of the gym and offered her a membership and she said she'd think about it because there was another gym that she was considering.

"Okay," I said. "Well, In the event that you don't like that gym, I'll sign you up for this one. And since you just moved to Philly and you don't know anyone yet, you'll have my number, you know, so you will have someone to call in case of an emergency."

I gave her a ring the next day and asked her if she would like to join our gym. She said she had signed with another place. And I'm not gonna lie, I was kind of bummed. I would have liked running into her at the gym and sharing another laugh like that. She is so funny.

Again, because she didn't know anyone in Philly and I also

enjoyed her company, we hit it off and decided to be friends. We'd go over to Marathon Grill, at 16th and Sansom Streets, which was right across from her corporate apartment. We'd sit, have a drink, and laugh. I'll never forget the night, while eating dinner at a Cuban restaurant in Rittenhouse Square, Teresa and I had this amazing, worldly conversation about everything in life. And towards the end of the night, I mentioned to her that I only obtained my GED and had a few college credits.

"What?" she asked.

"Yeah, I'm currently studying business at DeVry, but I don't have a college degree yet."

I felt proud because she thought I was incredibly intelligent and could not believe that I didn't have a degree.

Over the next few months, our friendship grew. It was a wholesome friendship; we'd take walks in the park, visit museums, go to concerts, see movies, play pool and attend the symphony. One of my favorite things to do was to go over to her apartment on the nights I wasn't studying, and she'd make these cute little salads and we'd sample different wines from around the world.

School was going well until I had a professor who seemed like he hated his job. You know the type - they think that just because they profess they should be treated as a deity.

We were working on a group project, which I never liked because I don't like hanging my success on other peoples' work. And for this reason: no matter how hard you may try, that doesn't mean the others in the group will try as hard. And just like that— our group failed. I showed the professor all of my individual work. I showed him the emails and everything. But he still failed me, and the administration was very difficult to work with. I went through the process of asking for a refund because the classes were expensive and I felt like they got over on me. The school was not easy to work with and I was angry. The customer service was horrible and every dollar counted for me as a single father.

That was a major discouragement on my path to getting a degree. And even though I did my part and worked as hard as I needed to—I failed the class. It was so shady. But let me set the record straight—although I left DeVry with no business degree, it wasn't because I gave up. I'm not a quitter. It's because I started to see them for what they were, not as a real university but as a cold-hearted revenue generating business! Also, another opportunity came about—just as I said they sometimes do and I needed the money to pay child support.

You see, in early 2007, I left PSC because Tommy Dellapenna, Perry Milou and John Andrulis opened a bad ass art space in Rittenhouse Square called Galleria 1903, and knowing my background as a pretty good sales person with the gift of gab, they asked me to be a sales consultant for them. It was a great creative space, which made it easy to say "hell-yes." It had amazing fluid energy and was rectangular with long wide walls. It really felt like a place to honor art, not just to make a transaction.

Things at the gallery were going well and I was proud to sell art full-time. And you know, when good things start happening and you're in the right mindset, all sorts of other good shit starts to come your way. I pulled my real estate license out of escrow and joined Weichert Real Estate, a firm just a few doors down from the art gallery and my friendship with Teresa was at a high. We were hanging out a few times a week and getting closer every minute.

Calvin Pierce, the best man at my ill-fated and highly secretive first wedding, called me up and said he was taking a business trip. Two of his kids from a previous relationship were in town and he wanted to know if I'd go stay at the house with his wife Heather and their two sons to help keep the 4 boys in line while he was gone. So I went over to Cherry Hill, New Jersey to help keep things in order for a few days. The four boys were fun and rowdy, and damn did they tire me out. You could tell I was a dad. And as dads do, I took a nap—it was on a Wednesday—and I woke up around two in the afternoon and Teresa was the first thing on my mind.

Hold up, wait a minute I thought! My friend of 6 months? It was a little weird that she was the only thing on my mind. So I called her and said, "Hey, I can't stop thinking about you."

"I can't stop thinking about you either," she said.

"Okay," I said. "Well listen, how about when I come back, I'll come over, you make one of those cute little salads and we'll have a glass of that New Zealand wine we previously critiqued, and then we'll kiss. And if there's a spark, we'll discuss it."

She thought that sounded nice, so I went over after I left Calvin's and Heather's house. She made the salad, we ate, had some wine, and then we kissed.

And sure enough, it sparked.

And sure enough, we did what people do.

And then we had a discussion. We were sitting on her couch in the living room and asked each other what our dreams, goals, and ambitions were. Where do you see yourself in five years? What do you want out of life? And you know what?, everything aligned. We both shared a passion for the American Dream. We both envisioned having a house and a spouse who would not only grow on their own, but that we could also grow with. We both wanted to be financially independent and travel the world one day.

We were both previously married for eight years before we divorced. We both had partners who were unfaithful. Even more serendipitous, my ex-wife's name was Danielle. Teresa's ex-husband was Daniel. There are a few other things that lined up perfectly but everything just felt... right.

And so, we named our goals and set things in motion. One goal we shared was to achieve a minimum net worth of $5 million together. That was a really big number to us back then. We knew it was possible, we both believed in each other's power, and we both believed in the possibility of manifestation coupled with prayer and action. We just wanted to build something special and to ensure that we were always on the right path, we took it slow and every step of the way, we were aligned, our goals were aligned, and our souls were aligned.

TWELVE

Mother Teresa

It was still 2007 when the company Teresa worked for was in the middle of a merger and, had it gone through, she would have moved to Milwaukee. By the grace of God, the merger didn't happen, so it seemed apparent that she was here to stay and that we just might truly be on the right path. And since she needed a permanent home, I told her that we could use my real estate license to help her find one.

And this was again pure kismet.

The townhouse I found her, the one she fell in love with, was at 731 South Hicks Street.

Teresa's birthday is 7/31.

I don't know, I'm sure people will say it's a simple coincidence. But given the serendipity of the other instances in our lives, I'd say it was fate. Mostly because Teresa and I, on paper, aren't really each other's type. But there was something special in our connection. There was something magical in the way we took it slow and were friends for six months before we started to date. So these little coincidences, we leaned into them. Because we believe in God. We believe that he works in mysterious ways. Que será, será-what is meant to be, will be.

And be it did.

Later in 2007, we traveled to the wine country and to San Francisco. We did the whole tourist thing and fell in love with Napa, Sonoma and San Fran. We even stopped by the first Williams Sonoma store. The founder has an amazing story on how that business was started and I have always been intrigued by it. A few days before we headed back home to Philly, we were walking on the beach in San Francisco and came across the most beautiful dog we'd ever seen. I remember saying to Teresa, "Oh my, I have never seen a dog like that before." We wondered what kind of breed it was.

Later that day, we saw two more just like it. It was a mix of a standard poodle and golden retriever. The breed was called goldendoodle.

By the end of that trip, we knew two things. The first was that when we retired, we were going to live in California. The second was that when we moved in together, we were going to adopt a goldendoodle.

In 2008, one year after our trip to California, Teresa and I decided to take our relationship to the next level. I said goodbye to Aunt May and let her know that I would check in from time to time. Teresa asked me to move in with her and I said, "Hell yeah, it was better than living in West Philly!" Her townhouse had a rooftop overlooking the city and we used to go up there with a glass of wine and chat through our daily problems. Always finding solutions together then moving on to gratefulness that we found each other. We have both been through so much shit in our lives that it was now comforting to partner with someone who was compassionate, empathetic and intelligent. Our friendship and love grew stronger each day because we made sure that we were always in alignment. By which I mean, we both knew what our dreams, goals and ambitions were, so we agreed as a couple, every step we took would be in a direction to achieve them. At our core, we wanted to propel each other forward and lift each other up to achieve success and a quality of life. This was in stark contrast to my past relationships where my partners seemed to have no interest in building me up. And I'm sure the same goes for Teresa. You see, before I met her, I was dating girls. This was my first experience dating and falling in love with a real woman who didn't need anything from me. As a matter of fact, I would say that she saved me and my kids. There is no way in the world that we would have the life we now have without her.

(Interesting tidbit, around this time someone sent her an anonymous letter in the mail. She read it to me, and we laughed about it, but it really hurt my feelings. Someone put in the time to look up my high school arrest record and sent her a copy trying to warn her about me. Either they were just trying to genuinely look out for her or they tried to purposely damage our relationship. Of course I already told her absolutely everything there was to know about me. We still have no idea who sent it.)

Living with Teresa was great. The kids were now 10, 13 and 16. When they would come to visit we would cook or go to dinner. Go to the movies or watch movies at home. We would sometimes take walks to Rittenhouse Sq. and life was really starting to stabilize for all of us. They say time flies when you're having fun. Well, the time came and sure enough, we did a fair amount of research before taking the kids on a road trip to a farm located in Oxford, Pennsylvania. After 10 weeks of waiting, we were finally introduced to our new goldendoodle puppy—a precious sweetheart we named Jasmine. She was the missing piece to our hearts.

We continued to take our relationship slow, letting life unfold naturally but every move we made was to get closer to that goal of a 5 million minimum net worth and closer to marriage. I knew Teresa was the one. So, I nervously asked her father if I could have her hand in marriage. He said, "Yes!" Then I asked him if it would be ok if I called him dad? He said, "Yeah!" I think it brought him joy knowing I was a good guy and I would treat his daughter well. Then, he went on to question where, when and how I was going to ask her.

Teresa was promoted from GC to President at her company.

She, and the higher-level executives were scheduled to take a trip to Aruba and since I was invited on the trip, I decided that while walking on the beach at sunset, I would ask her to marry me.

It was 2008 and our country was dealing with the economic downturn. Some companies were taking the government-funded TARP bailout money; Teresa's company did not. Consequently, she decided that it wasn't right for her President's group to take an expensive trip to Aruba during this time, so she canceled the trip. She announced that instead of the trip, they were going to save money at the company by cutting back on expenses.

"Well," her father said. "What are you gonna do now?"

I had no clue and Teresa had no clue that I was going to ask her to marry me.

I think Teresa sensed how bummed out I was because one night soon after, she said she had a timeshare in Ft. Lauderdale that we could travel to for spring break.

During the day she would work, while me and the kids would go hang on the beach.

What she didn't know was that we were practicing what would be one of the biggest moments of our lives.

Nightfall came, so we walked out to the beach to head to the restaurant for dinner. The sun had set, the waves were crashing on the beach, the bright moon was shining and reflecting off the ocean. Just then, me and the kids made a circle around Teresa. Holding hands, we all dropped to one knee and together as a family, we asked, "Will you marry us?"

"Yes," she said with an abundance of excitement.

It was, without a doubt, the most beautiful moment of our lives. To know that this incredible woman wanted to be a part of our family. My heart, our hearts were full.

A few weeks later, Teresa and I took a trip to South Carolina and on the beach, while the sun was setting, I got back on one knee and alone I asked if she would marry me just to be sure.

"I know the kids and I put you on the spot so, I just wanted to double check."

She said yes and we planned our engagement party, which her

father thankfully was able to attend. Her mother passed away in 2003, so it was special to have him around to celebrate such a beautiful occasion. After the party, I was blessed to have the honor of driving him back to his house in Virginia.

A few months later, he became sick and passed away before the wedding. Teresa says he died a happy man because he knew his only daughter was in good hands.

Our wedding occurred on July 10, 2010, at the Cairnwood Mansion Estate in Bryn Athyn, Pa. The forecast was a washout. Rain the day of and all through the night.

The wedding planner came to me and said, "I just asked Teresa this question, so I'm going to ask you too. Are we doing this inside or are we doing this outside? Because it's pouring down rain and we have about ten minutes to decide."

"Well, I can decide right now," I said. "We're doing it outside regardless, rain or shine."

"That's exactly what she said, now go get prepared, good man."

So, I went to my groom's room and popped open some Moët Nectar Impérial Rosé Champagne with my biological father and my son Devon, a couple of friends and a few cousins. Hampton was present but not present. He has always been emotionally vacant even before my brother died. I think a part of me wanted that day—that beautiful moment of my partner and I getting ready to be married to somehow snap him out of his unemotional stupor. But it didn't. It took me a while to realize, but he was a man who is entitled to be however he wanted to be and this experience with his son was not going to change that. No matter how badly I wished for it. Hampton would forever be my biological father who simply—could not express his emotions.

As we popped the champagne, the staff prepared the outside area, setting up the chairs and whatnot.

Then, as if the world was made just for us, the rain stopped, the clouds parted, and the sun came out with force and dried up the earth. Those cotton candy skies were so beautiful under which we exchanged our vows and said, "We do."

The next day, our daughters checked into Blue Tree; a girls empowerment camp held for two weeks in the summer at Bryn Mawr College. After which, they would stay with my mother in Norristown for a week. Teresa and I jumped on a plane for our honeymoon—Venice, Nice and Monaco, where we hopped on a ship and cruised the Spanish and French Riviera for two weeks. We came back to Monte Carlo for one night and had dinner at the Hôtel de Paris on her birthday. To say the trip was magical would be a cliched understatement. It was the greatest celebration of love and adventure we could have ever imagined.

The next day, we took a flight back to America and drove to Norristown to pick up the girls. When we arrived, Jordan and Alexis told us that the day before, someone was shot and killed up the street from my Mom's house—a stark homecoming reminder of where I came from. It was unfortunate news but I was thankful that I no longer lived there.

And you know, when Teresa and I first got together, she didn't have any children of her own. In her first marriage, she did have the chance to be a mother but miscarried. So, I told her that, if she did want a baby, I would be more than honored to raise a child with her.

"Let me think about it," she said.

The next day she came back to me and said, "Thank you for the opportunity. I love you but the answer is no thank you." Inside, I was screaming with joy because I would have made that sacrifice for her but I was so thankful she said No!

She had a stellar past in making great decisions, especially concerning the jobs she wanted to take. You see, before I met her, she had several job offers in different states around the country but she chose the one in Philly and we met a week after she moved there. I'm so happy we didn't have a baby together because raising kids is hard work and I had been doing it since I was 22. I felt like

I needed to focus on creating a career for myself so I could keep up with her and do my part. Teresa was already a corporate professional and doing well but she was focused on becoming so much more. With her career taking off to new heights, she said, "I don't want to bear any children of my own, but Lenny, I will dedicate my life to helping you raise yours. And when they're out of the house and we're empty nesters, we'll spend the rest of our lives together, traveling and seeing the world."

There was nothing we felt we couldn't accomplish, and here we were, together co-parenting. It felt incredible, to put it mildly.

Despite the difficulties that came with it, not once did Teresa ever bat an eye at the responsibility of being a mother to my daughters and son. You see, after Danielle and I split, she started to descend into drugs. For many years, she seemingly kept most of her shit together, but as time went on, things got worse, culminating in a situation where Alexis was about to be kicked out of her private school because Danielle failed to pay the tuition. And who was there to save the day? Me and Teresa. One weekend when the girls came to stay with us, they told us that their home life and their mother was getting progressively worse. She was stealing Lexie's phone, receiving and sending extremely inappropriate messages to men and getting some back, which led to an even more volatile situation. My beautiful, hardworking and intelligent daughters, now ages 12 and 15, asked if they could please come live with us.

Teresa and I had to make decisions on their behalf, as we wanted them to have a better life than I had growing up. They didn't need to be in a situation that would bring them down instead of building them up. We felt that living in that house with their mom, two uncles and grandparents would slowly destroy them and turn them into incapable adults like the other adults that lived there. We wanted to put them in top-level schools. We both knew that our daughters would need a good education if they were to have a chance at a decent life. We didn't want them taking the same path I did. We were determined to create generational opportunities to ensure Jordan and Alexis would never be uneducated or hungry. They needed a responsible adult to make those decisions for them.

So, we started looking for homes that had impeccable school districts.

No matter how good a realtor you are, finding the perfect home—a solid home that you're in love with—can be tough. It was the summer of 2009 when we started looking for the home in which we would truly begin to start a new chapter together. Over the course of months, we would put in offers on home after home, and each one would fall through. School time was coming up and I started to worry that we wouldn't find a home in time for the girls to begin classes in the fall of 2010. We even considered getting an apartment to qualify to be in the Lower Merion School District and then continue to look for a suitable home in the area.

I drove around this perfectly located and charming neighborhood called Penn Valley a few times. I decided to take one last drive through and if there was nothing, then I would head over to Gladwyne, PA., the next town over.

I drove past the Welsh Valley Middle School and made a left. And then something hit me—this powerful beacon of magnetic energy that just took over my body, mind, and soul. I've never felt anything like it before. To describe it, I would have to say it felt like an extreme giddy sensation with a burst of joyfulness and it guided me to the left. Then another left. And another. And when the urge to stop turning left finally ceased, there was this enormous home hidden behind overgrown greenery. The address was 324 Fawn Hill Lane.

There's no way we can afford that home, I thought, so I made the next right to keep driving.

I slowed down and came to a stop.

I realized it had to be the power of God that placed me there and I just had to go with it.

I pulled in front of the house, got out and just looked at it.

Always trusting my gut in real estate deals, I called the number on the sign, telling them I was in the business. I gave them my realtor security code and in turn I received the code to the lock-box. It was a little struggle to go through the overgrown grass and weeds as I walked up to the front of the house.

I unlocked the door, took a deep breath and then walked into the new construction mansion. The driveway was still gravel, no stove, dishwasher, freezer or refrigerator inside, floors unfinished, no light fixtures. No air or heat. Nothing. Cobwebs everywhere.

I walked the entire house. It was 10,500 square feet. I knew after strolling through, that sucker would become our home.

I showed Teresa the pictures I took once she got off work and asked her what she thought.

"It's unfinished."

"Yeah, but trust me on this one," I said.

When she got off work the next day, I picked her up and drove her over to see it.

After viewing the property, which was nearly 75 percent complete, she looked at me and asked, "Can you do this?"

The only full renovation experience I had ever done at this point was to my first home, Danielle's grandmother's home. I spent seven months getting that house ready to be lived in, doing most of the work myself. My aunt Ann and my amazing mother came down to help me on some days. With this new project, I would have to take a more strategic approach. I would learn how to interview and select the right general contractor to perform the work. The Lower Merion building code was strict and we wanted it to be done in the right way. And you see, when you're from Norristown, you believe you can do any fucking thing.

When Teresa's father passed away, he left her the house in Virginia that she was raised in. And because we knew we would be buying a crib; she had a real estate agent and close friend, Afreda Gordon sell the home rather quickly and we used that $200,000 as the down payment for the house. Otherwise, we would not have been able to buy it.

We put in an offer but, unbeknownst to us, the day prior, the builder was forced to give ownership of the house back to the bank before the bank started taking legal action against him for missing construction loan payments. In real estate terms, it's called a deed in lieu of foreclosure. The process allows the bank to take full ownership of the home as an asset and the builder walks away and keeps their good credit. Otherwise, the builder or home owner would receive a foreclosure on their credit when the bank takes back the house in a legal proceeding. Apparently, the builder had a few other homes he was in the process of building. He was still using the bank's money on those projects but they were in good standing. He made the right decision in letting that one property go before he destroyed his financial future. The home was listed for $1.9 million, but we only offered $900,000.

The bank countered with an offer to simply cover their fees. We applied for a mortgage and agreed to buy it for $1.1 million, and as we went on our honeymoon to Europe, our builder completed the house and we were able to occupy the home just in time for the girls to start school.

Unfortunately, their biological mother was not acting like a responsible adult. By this point her drug use deemed her incapable of making any type of long-term decisions. And so, Teresa and I wanted to pick up the slack and make all the decisions for the girls once and for all. Danielle and I had always split custody of Jordan and Alexis, but in 2010, after the girls came to live with us full time, I asked the courts for full legal and physical custody but child support was not necessary.

We wanted to be able to make the important life decisions for them and to travel out of state and country without needing to ask for permission from their mother every time. Besides, our goal was to get them to college and we would be the ones paying for it so we needed assurance that their future could not be sabotaged by anyone else.

All Teresa and I wanted was to give these girls the best life they could possibly have. We wanted to give them the head start that I did not receive. Living in this new home, they could have their own bedrooms, bath and space in a safe neighborhood with great schools. You know, the girls really didn't know that we couldn't afford to buy that house. We were living paycheck to paycheck, and deal by deal. We were certainly struggling but we could see the pathway to success. Teresa and I fully furnished the girls' bedrooms but our bedroom would have to wait. We slept on a mattress on the floor for a while. The house was huge and empty. We created a plan to finish one room at a time and after a few years, we finally had this amazing fully furnished home with impeccable landscaping and I designed it all. We bought the home under the assumption that it would increase in value. Remember, we purchased it from the bank for far less than it was worth. After we fixed it up, we instantly had about half a million dollars of equity. We could have flipped it and made a lot of money but we were focused on providing a solid foundation for the girls and giving them a feeling of living in a safe environment. We believe that education is everything. By the way, Teresa's mother was a science teacher, and we endowed a full scholarship in her name at the University of Virginia (where Teresa went to college.) It allows a black student to attend the school free of charge on a four-year education. It will do so in perpetuity. Education is important and we believe that having one is the first step to financial freedom.

It was a rough transition for the kids. We always had a great relationship with them but found out later, just before they moved into their new home, their mothers side of the family spread terrible lies about us. Initially and unfortunately the kids believed them. To make matters worse, when you live with a parent full-time—as compared to part-time when visits are a little more lackadaisical—things seem a little more strict. Dishes needed to be cleaned, rooms needed to be kept up, you know, basic chores and more discipline. As a result, there was some strife in the house.

It turns out that Danielle had been telling the girls that if I had full custody, it would ruin the good thing they had going, it would make her look bad and would hurt their relationship, and nothing would ever be the same.

And one day, the girls confronted me.

"Dad, don't do this to mom," they said.

And sure enough, the truth behind that behavior started to reveal itself.

During the custody hearing, Danielle broke down crying.

I requested a break and took her out into the hallway; her mother Marsha joined us.

"Why are you doing this?" Marsha asked, seemingly forgetting that her daughter was on drugs.

"Look," I said, "I am not doing this *to* you. I am doing this *for* the girls. Let me explain. Danielle, you have taken care of the girls full-time for many years. And I think you've done an okay job up until this point. Now it's my turn to have them full-time. You've had your turn with them. Let me see what I can do for them now. We have a stable family. We have a house in a safe neighborhood where they each have their own bedrooms and bathrooms. The kids are in great schools where they will receive an education strong enough to get accepted into a college that we will pay for. They each have their own group of friends. They are *stable*. Let's see what Teresa and I can do for them now. Because the ultimate goal is to get them into colleges, get them educated and graduated and out into the real world. Something you and I never did." Neither she nor I, went away to college and started a life of our own in that way. "I want them to be happy and to determine what success looks like for themselves. I want them to one day have families of their own."

Danielle was still crying and said, "It's very hard to deal with this." I told her, "I know in my heart, it's the right thing to do." You see, there is nothing more important than advocating for your child's best interest and their future, especially when you are educated. I know this because my fathers—plural—never did shit for me. My mother did the best she could and I am grateful for her, but the men didn't do one damn thing for me. Never did they advocate for me the way I wanted to advocate for these amazing girls. I loved them with every fiber in my soul and I was determined not to let them down. And to do that, I had to be tough with their biological mother, but I had to be compassionate as well.

"Danielle," I said, "I'm so sorry but you are an addict. You need to get your shit together. Don't you want to be involved in your kids' lives? In your grandkids' lives?"

"I do," she said. "I do, but I wasn't thinking that far ahead."

"You see, I am. And I *want* you to have a relationship with your grandkids. But if you don't change your ways, you won't even have a relationship with your own kids." I responded.

"You're right," she said.

So, we went back into the hearing, during which I received full custody of the girls. Unfortunately, Danielle didn't change her ways. We are still cautious of their interactions with their mother but they are now adult women who are very capable of protecting themselves. We do hope and pray that Danielle will be ok and that she turns her life around.

Thankfully, our daughters are very strong and intelligent women. Both graduated from college and are working adults. They exude the same resilience that I do. Even more interesting, Teresa is obviously not their biological mother, but the kids exemplify the same characteristics as Teresa—someone who I love and respect at the highest level. She grew up in a segregated school in the South. This is someone who dealt with severe racial issues in her community and overcame every obstacle that was placed in front of her. When I say she is tough and possesses fortitude, it's the least I could say. Furthermore, her ability to step in as the mother of my children when she certainly didn't have to, demonstrates what an incredible soul she is. She was the one tutoring our daughters in math while they were in school. She spent time helping them through tough social situations, took them to nonprofit events to teach them how to give back to the community, she took them to take the kids to work day and taught them about womanhood and life in general.

You see, together, we wanted each of our kids—and yes, we say *our* kids because Teresa has earned that role—to have it better than I did. In my entire family lineage, we had to fight. We had to be tough. We had to survive. And since I always wanted to be a father, my goal was to ensure that my 3 kids had a fighting chance in this world. Our goal, together, was to change the path of my family lineage so we would never have to struggle through financial hardship and starvation again. We wanted them to have plenty of opportunities and emotional support. We were able to help foster an environment where they could feel safe and thrive to develop their Intelligence, Perseverance, Discipline, Fortitude and Resilience.

THIRTEEN

Life Imitates Art

Real Estate will always be one of the best ways to make money in this world but when you service clients, you will need to swallow your pride sometimes. I made the transition from real estate agent to investor then to a developer because I wanted more control over my future and to make more money. I was lucky that it happened gradually and that I have a wife who was also my cheer-leader. We had substantial investments that we slowly made over time and Teresa received some hefty bonuses a couple of years in a row, not to mention her salary was increasing dramatically. We could see that we were on the right path and then some. There was this million dollar home in Gladwyne, Pa. that had been on the market for over a 20 year period with 10 different realtors that listed it at one time or another. The owners were very difficult to work with and the house was a piece of shit that really should have been torn down. The true value was the beautiful lot that the house was built on.

So naturally, the listing came into my possession and so, I listed it and then advertised and marketed internationally. You see, at this point, everything was going fan-fuckin-tastic. Teresa was crushing it at work. The girls were doing great in school. And I was selling million dollar homes on the Main Line just outside of Philly. We were thriving, inching our way closer to being financially independent.

Then I finally got a bite on the listing. A doctor and his wife, from Sweden if I remember correctly. And sure enough, the house was in contract to close and all the realtors in town started talking about me. I'd run into people at the grocery store next to our office and it would almost always kick off with, "Oh, you're the one who is in contract for that house that has been on the market for 20 years!"

I ate it up.

And then, I heard from the seller right after we closed on the house, who told me I should have gotten him more money.

"Hold on," I said. "What do you mean?"

"I know you were in fucking cahoots with the buyer. I know you and the buyer's agent went behind my fucking back and got me less money."

"Uh," I said, "The more money I sell your house for, the more money I make. What are you talking about?" Just then, I couldn't hold it in, nor did I want to. I had enough of his Main Line daddy's money attitude! I screamed "Fuck you and fuck your house, you bitch ass spoiled motherfucker." He said in a very soft voice, he was going to report me to the Pennsylvania Real Estate Commission. I yelled, "Be my guest you jackass and fuck off." On my way out of the building, I gave the celebratory champagne I was holding to the receptionist and smiled.

You see, no matter how far you get from Norristown, you're always one "fuck you" away because we don't let people talk down on us like that. Also, I didn't want to be in a business where I would be exposed to people talking down on me that way ever again.

When Teresa got home from work, I was fuming.

"Fuck that," I said. "I'm done with being a real estate agent. People think they can talk to me any way they want like I actually work for them. I work *with* people to help them with their real estate assets. I am not their employee. I don't work for them. Fuck that!"

"Okay, I got your back," she said. "What are you going to do now?"

I thought about it and said, "I'm going back to school and I'm gonna be an architect."

"Oh I like the sound of that." She said, because she is the most supportive wifey in the world!

The next day I typed "how to become an architect" into Google and Drexel University popped up. It was a good school and I learned they partnered with Montgomery County Community College (MC3) to make it easy for students to transfer. All of the credits I had thus far would be accepted so I could get an associate degree in fine art then transfer straight to Drexel. It would take many years but it was a great plan and very doable.

There were two professors at (MC3) who I got to know personally, (Holly and Roger Cairns.) We would hang out from time to time and we became good friends. I guess because I was older than most students and had a successful entrepreneur and real estate career. They thought I would make a good board member for the college so, one thing led to another, and the next thing I knew, I was parking my Range Rover in the faculty parking lot to attend my student classes in 2011.

Being a board member, as rewarding as it was, wasn't nearly as exciting as being a student. You see, there was something special about being an art student. It felt better aligned with who I was as a person. I allowed my soul to dive into this creative side of me that needed to be explored much more deeply. And I really got sucked into the creative aspect of it all. Sure, architecture was cool, but art was the foundation of it and it was amazing on its own—it opened doors to other worlds, to past worlds that I had yet to discover. I had some fantastic professors. It was very exciting to experience the many facets of art such as composition, techniques, methods and color theory—but I also got the chance to study art history. I enjoyed learning about the Caves of Altamira and the Paleolithic

Cave Art of Northern Spain. We learn about the Medici Family and their contributions to art and science. We were taught about Brunelleschi, Michelangelo, Dali, Picasso, Monet and the other greats. At first it was a little weird referring to myself as a painter and as an artist because I have many other talents, but at the end of the day, that's what I became. Although I still wore the hat of an entrepreneur, the particular hat of an artist fit just as well.

When I graduated with my fine art degree, It felt like a million bucks. Not only was I pursuing a passion that excited me, but I was also able to fulfill that promise to my grandmother. I told her I'd get my degree one day, and the day finally came when I got that fucking piece of paper.

Proud grandson scores another touchdown!

Now, I was going to put it to use. So, I shopped my art portfolio around to some galleries. I was so proud to be an artist and I was ready to put myself out there. Each of the galleries I spoke with wanted to represent my art, but they said they would take a 50 percent commission. And then I remembered—hold up, not only was I a seasoned 10 year real estate professional, but I had a very solid career as an art consultant selling fine art. I thought, why don't I just combine my talents and find a commercial space to show and sell my own art. I can do it all by myself. I can become a real estate investor and art gallery owner too.

I searched all over the Main Line, Philly, Norristown, you name it. I drove around for days and weeks but couldn't find a building that was ideal. I was determined not to settle for a 50 percent commission split. Then one day on my drive home, traffic was so bad on route 76 that I was forced to take a shortcut through this charming little town called Manayunk (Mani-yunk,) one of the western most parts of Philly. It's located right on the Schuylkill River (Skoo-kill.) You see, "Manayunk" derives from the indigenous Lenni Lenape word "Manaiung," a term for "River or place to drink." The Lenni Lenape Indian Tribe, of course, were the original inhabitants until selling land to William Penn.

As I drove through this town that had a great nightlife,

nostalgia hit. Something felt familiar. And then it hit me—this is where my friends and I would go to drink 25 years prior.

Right on the main strip, there was a raggedy building that looked like it was vacant, and it had "Bendi Jewelers" on the window, all faded out. Three doors over, another building had the same "Bendi Jewelers," on the front door but that one was obviously in business. I went in to speak to the guy about the other building.

Sami Bendi was the owner and one of the nicest guys I ever met. He told me that the woman who owned the other building was named Vilma and he gave me her number. Unbeknownst to me, Vilma was hard of hearing at eighty-seven years old. I called her and she answered, "Hello?" I said, "Hi, I'm calling about the building for sale." She said she couldn't hear me because she was old. So, you know me… I'm a solution-based thinker! I text her and we went back and forth until she was willing to sell me the building. We got a loan from the bank and bought it for $325,000. I gut renovated the entire building, investing another $125,000. The building needed so much work. Uneven floors, unnecessary walls, outdated plumbing and hvac and some structural issues. You name it but I was the man for the job.

On the first floor, I decided to put my art space—The Bazemore Gallery.

On the second floor, I remodeled the two apartments so I could get top dollar when we rented them out, essentially paying the mortgage so the gallery space would be free. All I needed to do at that point was rent the units at market rate and sell one piece of art per month to pay all the expenses for the entire building. My gallery was the best to have ever existed on Main Street and I was the first person to bring a living wall to Manayunk, PA. People used to come in just to see the orchids. In our best month of art sales we did over $50K.

We opened on October 5, 2013, and I designed the space based on the five elements of feng shui after consulting with a feng shui master in China the year before. I did this for good energy and prosperity. That's how I received the nickname "Zen Len."

I represented artists from Hong Kong, Philly, California, Italy and New York—all in this little, historic section of Philadelphia. I became a member of the Philadelphia artist community—a community that truly accepted me. I was able to thrive because I was free to be me, and as a result, I made Manayunk a better place. I sold a lot of art for a lot of artists. Not to mention I was able to sell my own personal art too.

One Saturday in 2014, Teresa surprised me with a trip to New York for my birthday. That was a workday for me in the gallery, so I closed the shop and vowed to open on Sunday since we were usually closed then. We got back from NY, and I rushed to the gallery and while I was mopping the floor, a man came to the door. I waved him in because he was just standing there. He peeked in and asked, "Are you closed? The sign says you are closed on Sunday." I laughed and explained to him that my wife took me to NY for my birthday on Saturday, so I was open on Sunday. He took his time walking through my beautiful gallery and then suddenly became more serious. Walking right towards me with his hand out, he introduced himself. "Hi, my name is Matt Callahan, I work as a Set Director and I'm with Touchstone Productions on Market Street. We are shooting a pilot for ABC and the new show is called "How to Get Away with Murder." I was bugged out by the title for the TV show. But he ended up leasing artwork from me to be used in the show. As you can imagine, I was extremely excited and couldn't wait to tell Teresa. She was the one that would help me to create the consignment agreement because I always went to her for anything relating to legal matters. I mean why not? She did graduate from Columbia Law School.

Teresa and I were so externally focused on our $5 million dollar goal, we forgot that we had a fraction of that sitting in the equity of our home. Some of our previous investment came through and on paper, we did quite well. So, we bought the building across the street from the gallery and opened a healthy organic restaurant called "The Juice Merchant." We bought two more buildings on the street using a loan from the bank. 4343-45 Main Street had eight apartments and two commercial spaces that we would buy for an incredibly low price and then fully rent out and hold for two years before selling and making a million dollar profit. We opened a dog bakery business called "Pet Friendly Dog Bakery" in another building we owned. At one point, we secured seven buildings on one block on Main Street in Manayunk, Philadelphia. (First black folk in history to accomplish this in that town.)

One day, I went back to visit Norristown and was chillin' with some of my childhood friends and one of them said, "So you own an art museum now?"

"Gallery," I said. "An art gallery."

"Yeah, yeah but what do you do? Do you show art or something?"

"Yeah. I show art. I'm a painter and created some of the art myself."

"Man," he said. "What do you know about art, you're from Norristown?"

And that was his mindset. To him, art was an untouchable world, he thought that people from Norristown, people from other poor communities—couldn't know anything about it. But who could blame him? You see, when you grow up needing to hustle just to survive—not even to become successful, but just to survive —your world is dramatically smaller, your opportunities are narrow. I knew from a young age that I needed to get out of Norristown because personally speaking, if I stayed, I never would have lived up to my full potential. I knew all those years ago that I possessed ingenuity. I taught myself how to properly eat at fine restaurants and to know what wine to order with food. I paid attention to other cultures and learned how to respect their ways of doing things. I learned etiquette and mannerism to become a cultured person. I understood the limited opportunities Norristown had to offer a creative person like me and, if I accepted that as my fate, I would be just another guy who thought art was untouchable. I would be just another guy, father of three, husband to God knows who, working two, maybe three jobs just to pay my child support, rent, and whatever else that dead end road would have been.

I came a long way but I still had some work to do. We previously had vacationed in Vancouver, Montreal and Toronto. We love Canada and so, Teresa and I took a trip to Quebec City for our 4th wedding anniversary. When we deboarded the plane and made our way through customs, we handed over our passports, excited to keep rolling through.

The agent, however, told us there was a problem and we would not be allowed into the country. Instead, they took me into a little room, without Teresa, my Columbia Law grad wife. The agent typed something onto his computer and pulled up an Interpol database.

"Is this you?" he asked, while pointing at the screen.

The computer said "Leonard A. Bazemore."

"Yeah, that appears to be me."

He looked at me and said, "You have criminality."

"Criminality?" I asked!

"Yes! He spoke.

In 1988, you were charged, arrested and received one year of probation."

WTF? Criminality? And then it hit me—Tony Buffa! The fight that got me expelled from high school and caused me to lose my football scholarship to the University of Pittsburgh. I mean Damn! It was now 2014! After that happened to me at school, I was so depressed, on drugs and alcohol and was hanging around the wrong people. I got into a little trouble afterwards but that was a case of being in the wrong place at the wrong time and being blamed for something that I did not do. Otherwise, I was a good dude and didn't get into any more trouble with the law.

An hour of being vilified and a $240 dollar fee later, I had what they called a special visa to enter their country and we were finally able to visit Quebec City. This left a bad taste in my mouth. Canada is beautiful and I did not let it ruin my trip but come on man! (I believe the authorities abused the Interpol database system to create a cash flow revenue stream for themselves or for their government. I would love to see where that money goes and how much they generate every year from that bullshit.)

When we returned to Philly, I hired the best attorney possible to clear my record because there was no way I was going to have that haunt me for the rest of my life. Consequently, I had to go in front of the Pennsylvania Board of Pardons to plead my case to be officially pardoned by the Governor of the state.

I told them everything. The truth and nothing but. Can you believe that after the incident in Quebec City, It took 3 whole years just to stand in front of them to plead my case because they were so backed up with other cases.

And after I finally spoke with the board, I was given a copy of an affidavit from 1988, the same one Tony Buffa swore to and signed all those years ago. My goodness, my heart stopped! His signature was right there!

Remember, back when I showed up to the preliminary hearing with my mother and uncle Nabop and that white lady came running up and told us that I should waive my right to a preliminary hearing, which is exactly what I did because we were uneducated about the court process.

Had I not done that, I would have heard Tony's side of the story.

Turns out, Tony lied to the school and to the cops. He said that he didn't know who I was before that day. He said he was on his way home and I just ran up to him for no reason and sucker punched him.

To make matters worse, he skipped school that day. Tony wasn't even supposed to be on school property. Yet he was. He was there to pick a fight with me because he liked my girlfriend Kathy, and as a result—if you remember— he spit on me, then he slapped me. He swung first, I walked away and then he tried that bizarre karate move and that's when I defended myself.

We could not afford an attorney and we were not educated on court proceedings and because that woman rushed up and said it would be wise to waive the right to my preliminary hearing, we listened to her. I suspect she was on his side but I don't know for sure. I went directly to trial because I was young and scared and facing fifteen years in prison. Had we not listened to her, and instead chosen the preliminary hearing, I would have had the chance to hear all of Tony's bullshit lies and I could have refuted it. And the witness testimony would have been heard. I truly believe the entire case would have been thrown out along with the charges against me. I would have been back to school sooner, I would have graduated on time, I would have kept my scholarship and played football at the University of Pittsburgh. Hell, I might have made it to the NFL or at least had some kind of professional career in sports.

But instead, that woman hurt our family's immediate future. I was scared and had no idea how to deal with the legal system so we were easily taken advantage of.

Just one more reason why the financial status of my family needed to change—it deserved to change. My family has struggled for too long for me to just stay in Norristown. I was suppressed by my circumstances and environment for too damn long. That's why every action I took was to propel me forward, and every decision Teresa and I made as a unit was to insulate our family and protect our interests and everything we worked so hard for. We are both educated now and have international attorneys on speed dial if anyone tries any bullshit from now on. Remember how back in 2007, that day Teresa and I decided to kiss to see if there was a spark? And when there was, we discussed our dreams, goals, and ambitions?

That number we came up with—the $5,000,000—that wasn't some arbitrary number. That was a number that we both said, almost at the same time. It was a number that both of us had already thought about on our own before we had the conversation. We both knew that we wanted to, at some point in the future, be worth at least that amount. So, when we realized we shared the same goal, we started working toward it. With every step we took in life, we had one dream. one goal. one ambition. Together!

One day, our daughters were in their bedrooms doing their homework and I was on the couch watching TV waiting for my beautiful wife to come home. I heard her pull into the garage and was excited to see her. Because you know, that's how best friends who are married act sometimes. We love sharing our day with each other and as she walks in, and before I could even say hello, she says, "Hey, I received amazing news today."

In Five years.

Every thought we made.

Every single move, every decision for five short years, built up to this moment in 2012.

Teresa and Lenny Bazemore officially became millionaires.

The little boy who had to boil buckets of hot water and lug them upstairs to the tub so his family could bathe.

Bullied because of the kerosene smell of his clothes.

Wore oversized used Nike sneakers to school, baseball practice and games.

Who had two fathers that turned out to be useless.

The young man who was stabbed twice and had a gun held to his head.

Who had shelter and food insecurity.

Who hustled and worked 75 different jobs.

Who wanted to live the American Dream and fly on a private jet while eating caviar and champagne like Nick Kimball and Dominique Devereaux.

Who persevered. Who persisted. Who was determined and relentless.

The young man who was resilient.

He and his supportive, loving wife—who he couldn't have done it without—had just become millionaires.

FOURTEEN

Blessed Beyond Belief

Fast forward a few years and the sound of becoming multi-millionaires has a nice ring to it. What finally pushed us over the threshold was our early investments and creating a diversified portfolio. You see, we made a lot of very intelligent decisions along the way. As with any investment, some took many years to come to fruition. As we built our relationship, we started investing early and did extremely well in everything. Such as investing in crypto, buying residential real estate that would appreciate in value, buying commercial buildings in Manayunk, Philadelphia then conceptualizing some businesses to place in the space. Turning them into revenue generating properties then selling at the right time. We became early investors in a software company 17 years ago. We invested in a perfume business, cyber security, storage facilities and other strategic angel investment opportunities that came our way. It was very important that we partnered with the right wealth advisor that could protect and grow our portfolio to new heights. All this in addition to me developing multi-million dollar real estate projects and Teresa's income from an impressive and prestigious career path that led her to appear on the Black

Enterprise's 75 Most Powerful Women in Business list. She is a badass and also on several paying corporate boards.

Life has been quite the journey as we trek down the road less traveled. Making money and then knowing how to make that money work for you is essential to building wealth. We're fortunate that I went to middle and high school with a good friend named Larry Gilston. At the time, Larry worked for a Family Office (Asset Manager) called the Lenfest Family Fund. They would go on to merge with the Forbes Family Trust (FFT) office out of New York.

He and I maintained a friendship for all those years and we would talk about investments from time to time. One day, he offered to come over and present some options for Teresa and I since we were close friends.

He said, "As of right now, we're only taking one or two clients per year, and you must have a minimum net worth of five million. Even though you don't have the five million yet, we see an upside to having you two as clients."

There it was again—five million.

It was in 2014 when Larry and Scott Gregorchuk, the Vice Chairman of the company (FFT) rang our doorbell. They gave us an expensive bottle of Caymus wine. We opened the vintage bottle and sat in our living room as we discussed our financial future over a premium glass of cab. At the end, Scott said, "Listen, you know—we don't take on clients who are less than five million. But because of your relationship with Larry, and because we see potential in you, we want to bring you on as clients and welcome you to the Forbes family."

We, very cool and collectively, said absolutely. Internally though, we were on cloud 9. Let me explain something to you: very few people get an opportunity like this, let alone a black family that didn't grow up with much.

And to be clear, this didn't just "happen" for us—this meeting with Larry and the relationship with the Forbes Wealth Advisors. This wasn't a coincidence, and it certainly wasn't serendipity. It was a combination of manifestation, prayer and action. Teresa and I believe that manifestation and prayer work. But without action, you will not get as far. There is a good chance that you will be in the same place going into the next year and the year after that and so forth. Teresa and I never think that we don't belong somewhere or that we don't deserve something we want. As a matter of fact, she always says, "Never self select yourself out of the process. Go after whatever it is you want. If you want that job, then go for it. Go through the process and let them tell you no! The worst thing that could happen is you gain experience by doing the interview." And even though she never played sports, she and I have the same mindset when it comes down to it. My version of it sounds like this, "In baseball or in life, the only way to hit a single, double, triple or homerun, is to step up to the mother-fucking plate and swing at the ball."

After I lost my college football scholarship, I could have simply stayed in Norristown and continued to pray that I would become a millionaire, that I would meet a beautiful woman, start a family, and one day magically end up in the Hollywood Hills. But it doesn't work that way. The reason Teresa and I are successful—is because with every prayer we send up to God, with every act of manifestation, we put in ten-times the amount of action. We identified the right people to network with. We formed in our minds the exact specifics of how we wanted our life to go and worked towards that goal. You see, we didn't just say, "We want to be millionaires." We put a specific number on it—$5 million. And with every step we took, that number came up again and again. With the help of Forbes and the additional investments we made outside of them, we realized that our goal number all those years ago was too low and we felt comfortable increasing it to a minimum of $50 million net worth. We are incredibly thankful for the life we live and we worked very hard to get here and see no reason why we should put a cap on it. We refused to allow our early childhood circumstances and our race to define our financial future. We are blessed to be born and raised in the great United States of America and we owe it to our ancestors to be the best we can be and take full advantage of every opportunity in this country. If you want something, you have to determine what it is that you want, be very specific and in detail with this power. Be brave and create a plan on how you're going to get it, be willing to pivot when things get tough, and then go get it while you can because years will go by quickly and being stuck in the same place year after year is hardly fun. Plus, you may not be here tomorrow.

In 2017, Teresa and I along with our youngest daughter Alexis flew out to Los Angeles to attend a Hollywood Hills house party to celebrate with Lin-Manuel Miranda for his success with *Hamilton*. We chilled with celebrities including Kobe and Vanessa Bryant. One of the most charming loving couples we ever met. Alexis actually taught Kobe what Snapchat was and did a quick video with him. Of course her friends loved that. We visited LA several times prior and always enjoyed it. But this time, something felt different. Being curious, we often drove around to look at some of the beautiful California homes because they were a different style than on the east coast. We would always talk about the ones we liked so after returning to Philly, we had one of those conversations where we had the same thought, but it was the first time we vocalized it to each other. Talk about relationship magic. As we aged, we thought that Philly was too damn cold in the winter, and it might be worth it to consider spending a few of those harsh freezing months somewhere warmer, such as California and maybe we could rent one of those cool houses that we drove past.

So, in December of 2017, at the recommendation of Teresa's cousin, Barbara Coleman, who lives in California, we rented a home in Santa Monica right on the beach for two months and it was incredible.

The Colemans are one of the most hospitable families you will ever meet. Barbara, her husband Wes, their son Wesley, his wife Jen and their 3 beautiful and intelligent kids, all welcomed us to California with open arms. When Barbara cooks, trust me when I say, you are in for a treat or should I say a delicious feast!

On the weekends, Teresa and I would drive around to see the multimillion-dollar open houses like on the TV shows. We'd walk through the properties, eat their hors d'oeuvres, drink their champagne and then roll the fuck out. Although it was just something fun to do, we really enjoyed meeting some new and interesting people. We also knew that one day, we would eventually like to retire and buy a home in San Francisco. And the only way to achieve your out of reach dream is to envision in specific detail what exactly it is you want. If you are yearning for a new car that's out of your price range or simply just your dream car, you better know the exact specifications. What's the make, what's the model, what does the exterior and interior look like, what year is it, what color is the trim, the tire brand, what kind of engine, how many miles on the odometer when you take possession of it—you better know it all and think about that fucker in every way possible. I mean, you must be able to describe what the leather smells like and physically see and feel yourself driving the car! When you do, what song is playing on the radio as you start to slow down at that stop sign. You just rolled down the window, what does the air smell like? You must fantasize with a vivid imagination like when you were a kid. Then, like I said, coupled with prayer and action, that shit just might happen!

We joked about one day having a house with a sick view of the mountains and downtown. We just knew that we'd end up in California someday but thought it was a long way off and dreamed that it would be in San Francisco.

After viewing the first house in LA, we discussed, "What if we bought a house right now? The property value would increase significantly by the time we were ready to move into it. And in the meantime, we could rent it out."

So, we put a timeline on retirement—7 years. By then, we could get everything in order on the east coast and the tenant would have paid us a lot of money in rent. So, when the time came around, we would move out to California and live in whatever home we purchased. So, we started to consider buying a house immediately and to our surprise, the conversation took a turn and we ended up discussing what it might be like to live in Los Angeles instead of San Francisco.

House number 2, 3, 4 and 5 were nice but not the style we were looking for. It became a real pastime. I mean there was no pressure on us at all. You see we already had a great life and two other homes on the east coast, and we weren't really that serious. House number 6 and 7 were too far out from LA because we like to attend visual and performing art events, walk around and dine at great restaurants. House number 8 well, that one had something. It was a Spanish 1920's style home with views of downtown LA, a swimming pool, nice tiered landscaping with orange fruit trees and it was in a great location. We didn't like the lower level because it felt a little choppy and tight. We like open floor plans with plenty of space. The house was vacant and staged but I recall seeing what looked like the owner's personal clothes in the walk-in closet. I noticed there was a toothbrush and toothpaste in the bathroom too. It did seem like he was staying there. However, we liked the overall house so much that we decided to come back to see what it looked like in the evening, when the city lights offer a different view of LA as the sun sets. We had a couple of hours to waste, so we drove around the hills. We turned and maneuvered through the curvy streets and up and up we went. We then came across an open house sign. The house looked so familiar, and I quickly realized the information sheet was in the back seat in the pile of open houses that I printed out that morning. I put it in the we can't afford it category but since we were parked in front and it looked like someone was still inside, even though the open house sign said it was over at 3:00 pm and it was now 4:00 pm, we decided to see if we could take a quick peek. So, the 9th open house we walked into, this realtor dude was sitting on the couch with his feet up like he owned the place.

As soon as we opened the front door, we were struck with a view of the mountains to the left and downtown Los Angeles centered right in the middle of the floor to ceiling windows. Picture perfect. We had never seen a house like this before. We made our way through the upscale home like an episode on MTV

Cribs! We ended up on the roof deck, which had 360 degree, uninterrupted views of Los Angeles. Embedded right in the Hollywood Hills, to the west, you can see all the way up Sunset Boulevard and Downtown LA. To the south, Baldwin Hills, (which is famously called, The Black Beverly Hills.) To the east, Beverly Hills, Century City, Culver City, Santa Monica and the Pacific Ocean.

We were smitten, and it felt like home.

As we came back downstairs, the realtor—Jason Oppenheim started telling us how he was in the process of filming a pilot for a new show called Selling Sunset. He said an agent in his office named Mary and her boyfriend at the time named Romaine, filmed one of their scenes in the house and kissed on the roof deck in the first episode. He went on to say that he was going to pitch it to Netflix in hopes they would pick it up. Well, Netflix did pick it up and it's now a very successful show. (I ended up on season 4 episode 4 a few years after, so go watch it and check me out.) We told him good luck with the show and then Jason said, "Hey, I'm not trying to be that guy, but the house has been on the market for a week, and we have an accepted offer. The couple should be coming in to view the house again in a minute and that's why I'm still here."

Indeed, the house had been on the market for a week, listed at $5.6 million, with an accepted offer of $4.8 million.

Just then, this stylish young couple came through the front door. So, I jokingly said to them, "Hey, congrats on the accepted offer. We didn't want this fucking house anyway." Everybody laughed, but there was a part of me that was upset. Somebody showed us something we loved and wanted, and then we were told we couldn't have it. We were bummed. We left the house, hopped in our rental car and talked about how brilliant of a plan we had. I mean really, we thought it would have been a perfect plan. And out of all the houses we viewed—and trust me, we saw 8 other beautiful cribs, all over Beverly Hills, Los Feliz, Pasadena, Encino, and out of all of them, this was the one. We would later realize through all our talks and joking around; this was exactly what we had envisioned as we formed this idea in our mind from open house 1 through open house 8. By open house 9, we found it and didn't even realize it.

So we stopped by a Starbucks, grabbed a coffee, then went by another open house—number 10. When we stepped in, the realtor greeted us, told us he was just closing up, but we were more than welcome to walk through.

"Thank you," I said. "It's a lovely home. How much is it?"

"$19 million."

"Whoa, no thanks. I'll see you later, have a great day."

But he was persistent.

"Come on, I know you can afford it, just do a walkthrough. I promise. Just take a look."

"I mean, it's a nice house," we told him, "but we can't afford it. Plus, the house we really wanted, someone just placed an offer, and it was accepted."

"Well, you know, twenty percent of the houses in escrow fall through here in the hills."

And you know what, that is all we needed to hear. Teresa and I called Jason and told him we wanted to put in a backup offer. He asked if he could represent us and we said yes. We were happy to help him double bubble the commission since it was his listing. (To double bubble means to represent the seller and buyer on the deal, sell and receive a commission on both sides.) He recommended that we put in an offer at the same price as the first offer—$4.8 million. The problem with the first offer is they had to finance it. Suddenly, a backup offer made perfect sense because so much can happen when you ask the bank for money. As we left the home after meeting the young couple, I recalled the husband was proud and excited but the wife didn't look as sure. Something seemed off. They were planning to raise a family in the house, and it's not the kind of house you want young kids in. It was right there on the hillside. If a kid ended up on one of the patio's or the roof, it would take one simple misstep over the railing to tumble off and straight down the Hollywood Hills, right onto Sunset Boulevard. Not wise.

And sure enough, after the wife brought in a feng shui consultant, the couple backed out. Obviously, she paid them off to get out of the deal, lol.

We were in our rented beach house on February 4th, 2018 in Santa Monica hosting a Super Bowl party. We watched the Eagles beat the Patriots and as soon as our last remaining guest walked out, Teresa shut the front door and my cell phone rang. It was Jason Oppenheim. I said, "Yo, what's up man?" "Congratulations!" He yelled.

"Congratulations?" I said. "Man fuck that, I may be from Philly, but I'm a Raiders fan."

"No, man, not the game! The house. You got the house! We gotta get started tomorrow morning. We gotta get through some paperwork, we gotta get a check over, we gotta close in thirty days —" and he just kept going on and on.

When I hung up, Teresa said, "We got the house, didn't we?"

"Yeah. Oh shit," I said.

"Yeah, oh shit is right," she said.

And then reality hit us. We had no clue if we could afford it or not.

We already owned two houses on the East Coast—our $2.5 million-dollar, 10K square foot house on the Main Line near Philly and our 3K square foot $1.5 million-dollar vacation home on the Eastern Shore in St. Michael's, Maryland. We wondered if we could afford it or did we just get caught up in the moment on some wishful thinking shit.

So we called our wealth advisors over at Forbes, who told us that it was not necessary to liquidate any of our investment positions because we had some cash. However, we were still about $1.2 million short. They worked it all out and helped us with a short term margin loan, and in March of 2018, we closed on our new LA home in 30 days for $4.8 million in cash. (A margin loan allows you to borrow against the total value of securities you already own.) Jason immediately found a tenant and we signed a one year lease for $27K a month to rent out our new home. We then jumped on a private jet and headed back to Philly.

Ten years after we sat on Teresa's corporate apartment couch and aligned our dreams, goals, and ambitions, we were way above the $5MM financial goal we set out to achieve. In 2018, we literally bought a house close to our goal number and now, almost 6 years later, it's worth $10MM and that's why I love real estate investing.

That little boy from Norristown scores another touchdown.

You know, I decided to write all of this because it was my time to heal from my lifelong trauma and I thought that maybe, just maybe, I could help a person or two who may be struggling through life. My story is one of resilience and I hope people decide to read my book to find a little inspiration. I truly believe that if I can change my life—a poor black kid from Norristown— then it's possible for someone else to change their life for the better too. If you believe you can, if you manifest, pray and more importantly, if you put in the action part, with a little patience, you can literally do whatever you put your mind to.

If you are reading this and you are in a situation like I was or worse, you should also understand this: Times are way different than when I was growing up. When I was a young person, we did not have what we now know as the internet. Social media is a great but powerful tool and sometimes what you see on there can also be a showcase of bullshit. It creates a clear picture of the haves and the have nots and so much of it can be fake or meaningless. Work on being happy with your own life. Do not give into envy because once you do, you instantly eliminate whatever happiness you could have had. Be proud of your own personal accomplishments whether big or small. I know people say it all the time but none of the material things in life really matter. And when you don't have a lot of nice things, it may be hard to see other people have nice things.

Again, nice shiny things don't matter in life. It can be hard to believe when people say that, especially because it's usually annoying rich people with money to burn who say it. But I promise you that it is true. Some people chase money and get it only to find out that it didn't solve everything. It's just a tool to use in life. Many people use it to have a better quality of life and to help others. And some people can be irresponsible and use it to show off and think they are better than others because they have more money. This story, although it may seem like it was all about me striving for wealth and security, that was only part of it. Another aspect of it was understanding that my ancestors went through hell while they vastly contributed in helping to build wealth for this country. It's about honoring their past by becoming something to be proud of because we owe them that much. It's about escaping poverty and cultivating a life of joy, peace, love and financial freedom. The Declaration of Independence says that we are entitled to "Life, Liberty and the Pursuit of Happiness." It's also about being a useful person in the world and making a difference in other people's lives too. My wife Teresa and I are proud to have a proven track record of socially and financially giving back in meaningful ways. My friend Jaime Shepard always says, "Let Your Light Shine." I agree with him 100%. I just want to let my light shine! You see, life is not about finding yourself, it's about creating yourself and it's ok to be authentic and let your beautiful light shine.

My life is about wanting to live my version of the American Dream. To be in a marriage that is supportive and providing a better life for my family and being the best that I can be for myself.

My story is a journey to feel safe in this world and to mature naturally on my own terms even though I'm a big kid at heart. Honestly, the money does not erase the pain and I will surely go through life having to deal with more bullshit but, I now have a few tools that I learned from Dr. Kelly, that will help me deal with adversity in a healthier way. I would love to share all of the tools I've learned with you but, I implore you to work with your own personal therapist because everyone is different. I do not believe therapy is a one size fits all process. We all experience different types of trauma and the external variables in society that affect us in life are very different as well. Therapy is not designed to fix people. It's available to us so that we can heal and move forward in this world and curate the kind of life each of us thinks we deserve.

When you come from a place of poverty, lack of opportunities, lack of male role models and racism, a place riddled with strife—you're bound to have some issues. And when that trauma hits you, the rest of the world doesn't matter. The only thing you're thinking about is taking your next breath. Because humans are designed to do whatever we need to do to survive. But, when that darkness comes in and surrounds your entire fucking life, you may think that you won't be ok. You may think no one cares. You may not be able to see outside of your feelings, and then the breathing gets hard again. Options feel limited and life seems a blur. And if you're coming from a place like that, chances are, you may not have the knowledge to free yourself. You may not have the willpower and clarity that I did. So, what you need to know—is that you are respected and loved by someone, you must not give up. Someone cares about you; you must look inward and take inventory of your strengths; and if shit gets so bad where you start thinking it's not worth it and the darkness is just too much, you must find the courage to simply ask for help. You are not weak. You are strong. You have value. If you're black, chances are you may be a little more hesitant to ask for help. Like me, you may have been taught to hide your pain, hide your embarrassment, and just keep moving on as if everything is okay.

I'm voicing to all of you now—please do not do that! Because that trauma may resurface and get the better of you at any time. It's always lurking, ready to strike. Reach out to someone immediately—a counselor, doctor, teacher, a therapist, friend or parent, anyone—and tell them that you are not okay. That's it. That's all it takes! "I. Am. Not. Okay and I need help." Just keep moving forward. With the proper help, you will start to identify some triggers and learn tools that will make your life more manageable. Tools that can assist you in dealing with the trauma and depression that will no doubt help you feel better. And over time, the pain will start to lessen. The strife will start to disappear and you may one day find yourself in a position to give some wisdom to another who may need help.

Again, therapy for me was not an attempt to fix me. It was simply my time to heal and most importantly, it gave me some tools to deal with the bullshit that life throws at me. If you focus on manifesting and prayer then take action to make those two happen, you will be able to see progress towards achieving your dreams or just simply getting better and finding peace. Now, it will take time. It's not an overnight fix. It may take you many years like it took me, but things will get better.

I hope this book will be your seed of encouragement to help you keep fighting for whatever it is you feel you want or need in life. If I can do it then you can too but only if you are willing to put in the work. Use my book as a tool in helping you push forward and onward to something good and productive. It has always made me feel better when I feel useful. I once overheard someone say, it's not about what happens to you in life so much as what happens for you. It's all just the building blocks of life. Start somewhere and don't stop until you accomplish your dreams, goals and ambitions. Hopefully, when looking back on it all, you will be old and gray and would have found a way to have a good life, in addition to finding a positive way to be useful to others. And remember, when you smile, try to smile from your heart.

Point being, I texted my friend Michael Rubin not too long ago to say thank you. I let him know that on that day all those years ago, he planted a seed by giving me a tool to use at my disposal and I still use it. Growing up, he was the first one to show me and our other friends the way to wealth through hard work and diligence, laser focus and surrounding yourself with smart people and I was paying attention. I let him know that it was he who gave me those "Personal Power" Anthony Robbins motivational CDs in 1996, almost 30 years ago. And I told him that I was bummed at the time because he didn't give me cash instead. He told me that he didn't think I needed the money, and said that he believed in me all along. It was nice to hear him say that he was proud of me and that he knew I would make it. I went on my life's journey battling depression and other obstacles and realized that "True wealth can be measured by how well you treat other people," because "Kindness is the new currency in building humanitarian wealth." Mike gave me the help that I didn't know I needed. Time with his accountant and the motivational CDs.

And that my friend, despite what I thought at the time, turned out to be priceless.

Just three months after buying and renting our house in LA, our tenant asked to be released from the lease because he couldn't afford it. He said that he was a YouTuber and the agreement that he made sharing the rent cost with 2 other Influencers didn't pan out so he couldn't stay. He said he was working with a 9 year old named Lil Tay and admitted to letting her film in our home as she went on to tell the entire world that it was her multi-million dollar house on YouTube. I told him that was not cool and so, we came to an agreement to let him get out of the lease early and our house sat vacant for 8 months. Teresa and I discussed renting the same beach house in Santa Monica for the upcoming winter. We then talked about leasing some furniture and just staying in our own house instead because it was empty. That conversation led to us discussing what it would take to move to the west coast for good. We decided to go for it and came up with a plan to sell our other two houses on the east coast. I sold most of my commercial properties in Manayunk leaving me with two businesses and two buildings on Main Street (I would eventually sell those as well.) Then, we donated our 10K sq. ft. investment property in Norristown to Habitat for Humanity. Teresa had already retired from her job and replaced her salary with positions on several paying corporate boards and could work from home.

Except for living with my grandparents for several months in Macon, Georgia when I was 20, and after living my entire life within a 25-mile radius of Norristown, I was watching the movers load up our belongings so they could be taken to Los Angeles, a little more than 2,600 miles away. And so, our family chartered a private jet so we could easily get our dog Jasmine across the country since she doesn't travel well. And just like Nick Kimball and Dominique Devoreaux on that old Dynasty TV show, we enjoyed champagne and caviar mid-flight, and it would be there, in the City of Angels, that we would have an opportunity to make more dreams come true.

Teresa and I settled in and opened another bottle of champagne to celebrate. While sitting on the patio feeling grateful, I realized that our house was up on a hill overlooking the town. I cried tears of joy because we were living the dream I envisioned as a little boy and the same one we discussed while sitting on her couch all those years ago. All of this would not have happened without her. Teresa, you are my guardian angel, and I love you more than you will ever know. Thank you for being with me all these years and helping me become the man I always wanted to be. Thank you for lifting me up the way God intended.

After a year or so of living in Los Angeles, my friend Taneshia Nash Laird told me she wanted to introduce me to someone. She partnered with this gentleman's production company for a film project and thought it would be good if we met. And just as my life goes, it was Richard Lawson, the brilliant actor who played Nick Kimball on *Dynasty*. The man on TV I wanted for a father. The man whose character I wanted to be like. The one who taught me that black men could be strong. They could be millionaires. They could fly on private jets and eat caviar and drink champagne. Before seeing him do it on TV, I didn't realize black men could do that because I had never seen it before.

So, we met for lunch in Beverly Hills. I told him the back story and said what an inspiration he was to me.

"All I ever wanted," I said, "was for your character to be my father instead of what I was stuck with. I don't need any child support from you now, but would it be okay if I call you dad?"

"Well," he said, "Of course you can call me dad." We both cracked up laughing and he asked his good friend Glynn Turman to join us. A brilliant man who I first saw in "Cooley High" when I was a kid. It was a fascinating lunch.

Life is different here in LA. It's beautiful and inspiring. The one thing I have learned here is that if you can dream it, it can absolutely get it done if you know the right people. I have never seen anything like it. Very impressive place to live if you can afford it. On the east coast, you are born with a chip on your shoulder and some built in defense mechanisms. People are more authentic and to the point. The West coast is on a different frequency and operates on vibes and energy. It takes some getting used to and it has been a life changing journey.

Speaking of life changing, I thought my fighting days were over. I was 53 years old when I had to swing on some fucking idiot here in an upscale part of LA. I hit him with a fierce punch that knocked him on his ass.

On August 11th, 2022, I was coming out of CVS at 4pm in the afternoon. The witnesses said that 3 guys came up from behind, 2 black and 1 white and brutally attacked me. They punched and tackled me, kicked then tasered me. I didn't see it coming and then BOOM! I did not feel one ounce of pain but heard and felt a powerful thud on the right side of my head. I experienced a huge bright but comforting light and the next thing I remember is waking up, laying there on the concrete looking up at the garage ceiling. I remember taking this huge breath as if it was the beginning of my life. You know, the same type of breath a newborn would take when they first come into the world. Over and over, they punched, kicked and tasered me while going through my pockets.

I tried to stop them as they went through my pockets, but they kept hitting me. I could smell my skin burning from the taser on my right leg and at first, I had no idea what was happening to me. It all transpired so quickly in broad daylight and in a public space. I didn't understand what the situation was.

Then I heard a voice scream, "Give me the watch." At that point, my brain had a frame of reference. I was being robbed! Luckily, I was able to get on my feet even though they were constantly pounding me. Again, a voice demanded I give him my watch. I felt that my life was in immediate danger and I had no way out. I was slumped halfway over beaten and battered. His sneakers were to the left of me. I acted like I was taking my watch off but instead, I raised up and hit dude with everything I had. A fierce Mike Tyson style uppercut to his face and yes, I fucked his mothafuckin' ass up!

I could see his feet come up off the surface, he stumbled backwards, screamed like a little bitch ass punk then dropped to the ground. I didn't realize there were two other guys behind me but when I shifted my weight and pounded dude, instinctively I was able to run a few feet away to get clear and reassess the situation. I was now ready to throw down and fight for my life but when I looked back, I saw him crawling on all fours to get into the getaway car with the other two punks then they drove off.

The cops just happened to be across the street and came right over and asked me to file a report. In my opinion, West Hollywood Police get an F for effort because they said they are overloaded with cases and basically dropped mine like a bad habit. They even had information on who owned the getaway car and the house that it was registered to. They said they knocked on their door and asked a question or two but didn't arrest them or bring them in for further questioning. They also said the LA Sheriff's Dept will handle it but I haven't heard a peep from anyone. I was rushed to the hospital for a full evaluation. I was banged up pretty good for a few weeks but made a 100% recovery. I feel like the Po-Po blew me off when I attempted to get any information on the progress of the case. You see, when you deal with the police and you are black you sometimes wonder that if I were white would it have been the same outcome? Would they have put more effort into catching the dudes? Honestly, all I can say is that I am blessed to be here and lucky to be alive once again. Thank you, Lord!

For I am resilient.

Despite that one bad situation, we love living in California and people ask us all the time if we would ever move back to Philly.

Well, we miss some friends, the Philly culture, my mother who I see at least 5 or 6 times a year and other family but the answer is no. There are so many other places to experience and live. Why would I move back after I fought so hard to get out of there?

As a play on words from something my artist friend Justin Y would say, "I have seen the world in all its glory." Dining at Jules Verne in the Eiffel Tower in Paris. Touring Buckingham Palace in England. Driving through the French countryside. Teresa and I enjoyed dinner with Prince Edward and British Ambassador, Sir Peter and Lady Westmacott in Philadelphia once. Courtesy of our friends Oliver St. Clair Franklin, CBE and his lovely wife Dr. Patricia Mikols. We felt the power of the Iguazu Falls in South America and Victoria Falls on the Zambezi River between Zimbabwe and Zambia. Cruised down the Rhine River passing by the legendary Lorelei Rock and medieval castles in Germany. I panned for gold in a stream in New Zealand. Cruised the Yangtze River in China. Walked on top of a volcano in Antarctica. Out of breath on The Great Wall of China. Drinking wine and sunbathing on a nude beach in Hawaii. Speeding at 170 mph down the Autobahn in Germany. Seeing the Big Five while on safari in Africa. Practicing with a professional Sumo wrestling champion and then enjoying a traditional tea ceremony in Japan. Sipping on champagne in a tuxedo then having dinner while in Monte-Carlo at the Hotel de Paris and having lunch in Slovakia once, just to name some of our experiences. It's so funny to think back to my childhood because at times, I had to eat my breakfast cereal with water because we had no milk and when Teresa was a kid, she loved eating cereal but refused to drink the leftover flavored milk afterwards. We have both come a long way and are proud to say that we have enjoyed learning while traveling and exploring on all 7 continents.

Epilogue

My son Devon was an amazing kid growing up. He was funny, kind, creative and intelligent. We always thought he would do well in college when he attended. Maybe even become a scientist or doctor. He was so good at figuring things out and I was proud to see him develop into a solution based thinker like me.

Unfortunately, our relationship took a turn when he was around 13. His mother Kathy didn't tell me that he was starting to experiment with weed. He was hanging out with his neighborhood friends a little more and stopped coming to visit me on a regular basis when it was my weekend. I would call to schedule a pick up time and she would create excuses for why he couldn't come down for his visit sometimes. 2 years later, when he turned 15, I was finally notified that he was smoking when she put him in rehab without discussing it with me first. No plan of action to ensure we were all on the same page and no communication, just secrets. All I remember is her instructing me to pick up our son on Wednesdays from rehab. That is how I found out about it. Her actions were very controlling and deeply concerning as usual because there was no discussion and she left me with no choice. She was going to be dropping him off so, it was either I pick him up or he needed to find a ride home on his own somehow. I had a bunch of questions about why was I not told about it sooner and why on earth would she keep me in the dark about something like that. I wanted to know why she would try to replace me with her husband since I was a responsible father in his life. Keeping secrets is not good when it comes to a child. I voiced my feelings about raising him together. We were able to resolve the issue but it seemed like she was trying to get rid of me as a father even though I was dedicated to our son from day 1. She and her husband had two other kids of their own. I guess she just wanted my child support and not my valuable contributions in raising our son.

In 2008, Devon was kicked out of his public high school for God knows what and also out of his stepfather and mother's house for smoking weed and being defiant to his stepdad, so he asked if he could come live with Teresa and I.

Since I literally just moved in with her, I made him ask her personally. She was nice enough to say yes and because we valued education and wanted him to thrive, I drove him around to visit several private schools and then asked him which one he thought was the best fit for eleventh grade. He told us he would like to attend Valley Forge Military Academy (VFMA,) a prestigious military academy and boarding school designed to help young people on their path to adulthood.

It was a live on campus full-time situation but we agreed that it was the best fit in order to teach him more discipline and give him the structure he needed. I couldn't afford the entire tuition by myself at the time. So, Teresa was a savior and helped me pay the $35,000 tuition with monthly payments and off to college prep he went.

It started off like a dream. For the first time in his life, he received straight A's. He was talking about when he gets to college and his big plans for the future, and when he'd call, he seemed proud, content and happy. We were very pleased with the quarterly check-ins with the school. The discipline and structured setting was just what he needed. It was a little tough protecting him from the outside world because although Teresa and I were the ones paying the enormous tuition bill, we were not allowed to restrict other people who could visit him. They said that since we didn't have full legal custody, they didn't have to notify us when his mother Kathy or anyone else came for a visit. Mind you, I was still in court fighting with Kathy to end the court ordered child support payments she was still forcing me to pay even though she had already kicked our son out of her house. I had to hire an attorney just to get it dismissed out of the system and trust me when I tell you it was a fucking battle. Teresa and I wanted to reward Devon with trips to NY, different sporting events in Philly and concerts as a break from school. We asked every week if he could get off campus to visit with us. He would constantly say something about how he needed to earn a certain number of merits—earned by good deeds around campus in addition to good grades and a few other variables—which he said he didn't possess so he could not get off campus. However, we were able to take him to a Lil Wayne and T-Pain concert in Baltimore once. Also, a Philadelphia Eagles football game for his birthday.

A hard working kid, we thought. We could not have been more proud. We visited with him on campus throughout the year and although he was still a minor, the school never bothered to notify us that he was checking out to go visit people off campus.

And then we got a call with just two weeks left to go until the end of the school year. Devon was in the middle of taking final exams when he and another student were caught texting in class. The teacher confiscated their phones and when another message came in, he read it. Since they were texting about marijuana, they were immediately taken to the school's medical lab. Both tested positive for weed—a fast-track to expulsion at VFMA because of their zero tolerance policy.

It took a while for the real story to shake out, but that is usually the case with teenagers. Turned out that his mother, Kathy —who kicked him out of her house for disciplinary reasons including smoking weed, seemed to be jealous of the fact that he came to live with us and that we could get him into Valley Forge. She was picking Devon up from school during some weekends and taking him back to the same environment where he got in trouble in the first place and not once did Devon, Kathy or VFMA notify us that this was happening. A whole year had gone by and Teresa and I were left in the dark.

Let me be clear! Devon was the cause of this fucked up situation. But Kathy? She played a huge role in it too as an irresponsible parent. Teresa and I were on the phone with the school trying to make sense of it all. They said that after a review, Devon was in fact expelled from school with two weeks left to go in the eleventh grade. We called Kathy on speaker phone to get some answers. She was so fucking nasty and spiteful to Teresa and I. And as soon as I said hello, she said with a vindictive sarcastic tone, "Well, I guess Valley Forge worked, didn't it?" She then hung up on us. I immediately thought, how in the world could a mother sabotage her kid's future like that!

At the center of some of my young life problems—the fight with Tony Buffa and subsequent arrest, begging me not to leave Norristown to play college football and depression was Kathy. And here she was, appearing to be a major factor in our son's problems too. It broke my heart as a father because I only wanted the best for him. Despite my two dads, I always said I was going to be a damn good father and my kids were going to have better opportunities than me. But here was my son getting kicked out of a prestigious academy that Teresa and I struggled to pay for.

Although that was a pivotal time in Devon's life, there were countless times since VFMA that my son just couldn't get his act together but let's fast forward to October 2019. After a call from Devon who said he was finally clean and off drugs, I bid on a charity item and won a chance for him to work with a famous music producer in LA to create two songs. Since he still had his dream set on being a rapper, I thought I'd provide another opportunity for him to succeed.

I invested money in his music career before. On several occasions, I suggested that since he loved music so much that he should consider going to college to learn everything he could about it. I also said that if he went to school that he could probably use the campus music studio to make music for free. Then he could take his education and knowledge and apply it to a career in the business. He said that he didn't want to go to school and he just wanted to focus on making music. I wanted to be a supportive father and not shit on his dreams even though I didn't like his plan. He did have some talent as a rapper but I thought he should have a back up plan such as a 9 to 5 to pay for living expenses, just in case the music thing didn't work out the way he thought it would. I leased a professional artist studio space for myself and with the extra room, I built out a music studio where he could create his music and produce other peoples music too. I gave him the business model blueprint to make money charging for sessions but soon after, the landlord kicked us out because he and his friends were smoking weed in the building. Our studio was next to a little kids dance studio so the smell traveled down the hall quickly and a lot of parents complained. That was embarrassing! In the past, I gave him money for two CDs to be created and produced. Also money for marketing and album covers, only to find out he tried to flip that money on the street instead of its intended use, landing him in jail for a while.

I called Devon to tell him about the trip since he said he was drug free.

"We'll fly you out to LA," I told him over the phone, "and you can stay at our house."

"Oh shit, that's crazy. Thank you, Dad. I appreciate it," he said. "How much did it cost?"

"Well, uh, the whole trip and experience cost around 10 grand."

There was a pause.

"Why don't you just give me the money?" he asked. "I'd be able to do a lot more with it, you know?"

I was furious at how ungrateful he sounded. His mother has never done a fucking thing for him. He said "She basically doesn't even want to talk to him and rarely picks up when he calls." Here I was providing amazing opportunities for him to advance his life and follow his dreams.

I told him, "I will never again directly give you any more money because you can't be trusted to do the right thing with it. I told him that he was financially illiterate and doesn't understand the value of money even though I know I taught him better. If you don't want the trip, let me know and I'll just give it away to someone who will genuinely appreciate it."

After some back and forth, he finally agreed to come. He arrived in LA and the first few days of the trip went well. We made it to the music producer's studio and worked on some high energy music.

But on the last day of the trip, he went to a weed shop and came back with all sorts of marijuana products. He obviously lied to me about being clean.

"Devon, it's your last day here. You can't smoke all that shit in one day and you can't take that on a plane. You fly out tomorrow morning."

"What do you mean?" he asked, somehow unaware of federal drug transportation laws.

Even though it was his 3rd or 4th time visiting California, I explained to him how it was illegal and eventually we sorted it out, but the fact that he was willing to spend so much money on weed when he was broke AF, made my stomach turn. Setting financial priorities is incredibly important when you are not making a lot of income. Here was my son, behaving irresponsibly yet again with money. I am a supportive and patient parent and I don't care about anyone smoking weed but damn! I did everything I could to set him on the right path to being a good man. Being in his life constantly and showing him how to treat others with grace and respect. I taught him what it means to have a good heart and how to take pride in the things you do. Basically, how to be a good empathetic human. I made sure he received a good education including financial literacy. Showed him what it means to be responsible. Taught him hard work and ethics. He ended up dropping out of high school to get his GED. He enrolled in community college and dropped out. Then he went back and dropped out again. More of my money down the drain. All I wanted was a better life for him so it was hard for me to witness him being stuck. Hard for me to witness him not willing to put in the work to make his future better. He was there and saw me struggle financially and never give up, or so I thought. Maybe I did a better job of hiding it from my kids than I realized.

From time to time I would highly recommend that he work with a life coach or try therapy but he never did..

During his last day in California, Devon and I were up at Griffith Observatory checking out the amazing LA views when his negative attitude began setting in. I could see it happening, like when you can hear and see the rain start falling a few blocks away, but it hasn't reached you yet. So, I told him it was time to leave. In the G-Wagon, driving down Sunset Blvd, passing palm trees and feeling the sun radiating life, out of nowhere, Devon started crying.

"What's wrong, man?"

It made me sad to see him cry.

"Take a deep breath and tell me what's wrong bud."

And then it came out like a flood. "I gotta go home to a fucking shithole. Where I live is a fucking shithole. I hate living there. I can't understand why I can't live where you live. I can't understand why I can't live like you. Why can't I have what you have."

"Well," I said, and trust me, I told him the same motherfucking thing countless times before, "You can't cry over spilt milk. You refused to listen to my wisdom as I guided you through life. You made all those bad decisions on your own and now you are suffering the consequences." In my mind, there was no reason he should be failing in life because I gave him "The Blueprint" like the great Jay-Z gave the world back in 2001. My valuable words of instruction on how to advance in life never seemed to penetrate his brain because he was always looking for a shortcut. In life you have to plan and strategize at every level and be willing to pivot when things don't go your way. When you are chasing goals, you have to continually take inventory of what works and what doesn't work. Do more of what works but write down what doesn't so you don't keep making the same mistakes over and over. Also, it's good to keep inventory because if something doesn't work at one point, it doesn't mean that it won't work for you some time in the future. I never had a father in my corner that could give me play by play instructions on how to succeed and here he was wasting all of my hard earned wisdom because he thought that I should just give him the money and the lifestyle without earning it.

Again, I suggested that he might benefit from therapy, and that he would have our full support. With him though, it was always the same old shit with no progress. "Sounds a lot like constipation to me!"

It was through my sessions with my therapist Dr. Kelly, that I realized how much time I've spent pissed off at the people involved in the setbacks of my life—Kathy, Tony, Lark, Danielle, JB, Hampton and a few others. I spent a lot of time cursing their names and wishing I had never met them. It was an immature reaction the way I refused to take responsibility for my own life. I thought Kathy was the reason I never played college football. I thought JB and Hampton were the reasons for so many other things. And while there is an element of truth to all that, at the end of the day, I am responsible for myself, my experiences, my wellbeing, my reaction to things in life, and overcoming all obstacles. I am responsible for my failures and my success. I taught my son that he needed to take responsibility for his own actions and decisions in life too.

All the moments where I stumbled in life, it was because I got comfortable. I had to learn how to make better decisions and to be more productive. I fell several times on my journey but I was determined to fall forward. To be resilient. In a way, those people did me a favor when they fucked up my shit. One of the greatest lessons I learned from Dr. Kelly is that none of them can claim my prize. I entered the race and at the start of the gun, I fell a few times but I always got back up and kept running. I ran my ass off and lasted long enough to realize that I was in a race all by myself. I never had an opponent. As I stand on the championship podium of life, I realized that I became successful in spite of them. And despite all those people and their actions, I still fucking made it. I became more successful than I ever could have imagined and I'm just getting started.

The best part? I can see the big picture now; I can see how all of the misfortunes led to strength and greatness and for that, I am so very thankful. To all the people in my life who have done me wrong, thank you! Not in a passive aggressive way, either. From the bottom of my heart, thank you because I had to learn how to be a champion again. I had to learn how to forgive you and how to forgive myself.

"You are where you are now because of yourself," I said to Devon. "No matter what, you need to make better choices and those decisions will determine where you will be five years from now. You must put in the work because life ain't no get rich quick scheme bro. I made decisions to get to where I am today but I first had to accept responsibility for my own life. I had to take control over my own life. There's a distinct difference in how you live and how I live. I've earned all of this because I've worked for it and I am not willing to just give you the same lifestyle because we are related. How you currently live is a direct reflection of you not following my guidance in addition to your bad choices so, don't be mad at me because you gotta go home to a fucking shit hole." Sometimes people think they are movers and shakers. So busy trying to look like they are getting shit done but progress isn't progress if you are moving in the wrong direction!

The thing about advice is that it's kind of hard to take when it's unsolicited and you are a narcissist. Devon was still pissed, so we did some more sightseeing, went to the beach, and then I took him to a nice dinner in hopes that we could at least enjoy the last night of his all expense paid, first class trip on my dime. I went to the bathroom and called Teresa to tell her about Devon. She said, "Baby, he's only there for one more night. You can get through this."

He stayed quiet throughout dinner. I looked over about halfway through and saw how miserable he was.

"Here we go again." Any minute I thought…. And soon after,

he blurted out, "You think you're a good dad, but you're not a good dad."

There it is! Same shit, different day!

"Listen, Devon. Let me enjoy my meal. We've already had this same argument 20 different times over the years dude. You say I'm not a good dad, blah, blah, blah. Well, next month you will be 30 years old. I'm the one who's been there for you your entire life. You and your mom don't even speak to each other and you guys have no relationship at all! But let me ask you, Is she a good mother? What has she done for you? I have sacrificed my early life for you. You're out of your fucking mind to even think that I'm not a good dad. I'm a great dad. You know it. I know it. And everyone that we know, knows it. So stop what you're doing and get yourself together. Also, I can tell that you are high as fuck right now so, finish your food and change your mood."

He was still pissed because he couldn't get his way with me, so we finished the meal and left. When we got back to my house, I told him to pack up his shit because I was taking him to stay at a hotel. I didn't want him staying in my home that upset and while on drugs. My home is my sanctuary. A peaceful place where I lay my head and his energy was awful. I asked him to go get his things and said I would be driving him to a hotel down by the airport right away. Despite his protest. I dropped him off and went home to sleep in peace.

The next day, I answered his apologetic phone call. "Look man, I accept your apology and thank you for saying that I'm a good dad but I already know that I am, and I don't need any validation. I learned how to be a good dad by not having one. It is what it is dude. I love you and wish you nothing but the best. I hope that you seek therapy to make your life better." I was very angry with him. I refused all of his calls after that because it had clearly been a toxic relationship for quite some time and he had no interest in going to family therapy to find common ground, maybe learn a few tools to heal or even just to communicate better. And for me, therapy is essential and I have to protect my peace.

It was almost two years later when my mother called to tell me that Devon and his girlfriend were 4 months pregnant. (Ironically, while sitting on the front porch at my mom's house back in the day, she told me that Kathy was 4 months pregnant with him as I was preparing to leave for college.)

So, I called his cell phone.

"I hear you're having a baby"

"Yeah," he said. "Dad, I'm so sorry. I'm so sorry! I just want to apologize for my behavior in the past. I was wrong. Please don't ever not talk to me again. I need you in my life."

I forgave him but said we needed to complete family therapy together so we could heal from the toxic past. We talked about what that would look like in order to move forward. We discussed what it would take for him to stay drug free, healthy and stable, and what else he would need to do if he wanted to stay in my life. I told him that we could try to move forward because I wanted to be able to teach him how to be a good dad to his son. That was very important to me. We talked about how crucial it was to not stress out the mother of his child during the pregnancy. He seemed to be doing all the right things and when the baby was born, we thought it would change his life and that he might get on the right track. We flew them out to LA so we could meet the baby before he could walk. We spent time with them on the east coast on several occasions and flew him and the baby out to California again when he was going through a tough time with his girlfriend.

I was in my son's life providing for him since day one. I was the first to hold him when he was born. I did my job as a parent and filled his world with an abundance of love and guidance. I did the right thing as a young black father so it was very sad for us to see him and his girlfriend not perform their duties the way responsible parents should. Over the next year, our relationship would sour, mostly because he would not complete family therapy with me or even try to participate on his own. Through our years of discussions, I believe he also needed to work through his broken relationship with his mother. It never served him well when he would call me to start arguments because I refused to write him a check so he can live the lifestyle that we do. I also refused to invest in a clothing business that he created. Again, in the past, I offered to pay for college twice and he messed that up. I gave him a job at one of my companies and paid him well as an assistant manager and he messed that up twice. Paid for part of his music career because he said that was his dream and he messed that up. Helped him with 5 or 6 apartments and he messed that up by getting evicted each time because of not paying rent. He refuses to get a job and claims that he will never work for anyone else. He refuses any kind of mental health support and now lives in the heart of one of the worst neighborhoods I have ever seen. After the baby was born, Teresa and I were willing to provide a pathway for him and his new family to own a home in a clean and safe neighborhood but they refused to work a reliable 9 to 5 job to help pay for it. At some point, we shifted our focus to just providing some help for the baby's future but without directly giving them any money. We offered to pay for our grandson's education starting in daycare and all the way through college with their permission. They happily agreed and all together, we were able to enroll him into a $500 a week private preschool in Philadelphia where they would feed him nutritious meals and teach him English, Spanish and sign language. 3 weeks later and although I live in California, I received a few calls from the preschool asking if he was going to start school. My son and the mother of his child never communicated anything to us. They just never took him. When we finally got in touch with them, they complained that the 3 mile journey to the top rated school that we were paying for was too far and so they decided to put him in a nearby neighbor**hood** daycare with no curriculum. Teresa and I were absolutely disgusted at the lack of caring about the baby's future but there was nothing we could do. We argued with them about the importance of a great education and how valuable it is when you receive one, especially when you are a person of color. They didn't seem to care about it and we have not spoken since.

I would like to see Devon achieve measurable progress in a

reasonable amount of time. Therapy should be part of his plan to evolve. Hopefully, he can get his shit together for the sake of his son before it's too late. If anyone knows what it takes to sacrifice for your kid, it's me!

All I've ever wanted to be was a good father, husband and friend. I wanted to be able to talk to my kids and be there for them the way I wished JB and Hampton would have been there for me. I wanted my babies to rely on me, to smile, to share their dreams, goals and ambitions with me. We want them to respect us, to love us and in return, we want them to feel respected, loved, and supported. We want them to feel safe in this world. We want our kids to find their own way through life with our guidance and we want them to know they have rock-solid parents they can always count on. As for Hampton and JB, I forgave them for their absenteeism and abandonment. JB has since passed on and Hampton is still living in Delaware. We don't talk anymore because I stopped calling. What's the point? There is no emotional connection on the other end of the phone anyway. The last time we talked, I offered to pay off the mortgage on his house and he said no thanks. Even after all of my accomplishments, I used to feel like a little kid on the phone waiting for his daddy to say, I am proud of you son, and I love you. I never heard those words from J.B. or Hampton and can honestly say that I'm finally ok with that.

I spent my whole life looking for a father figure. I woke up one day in my 50's and looked in the mirror. The man I saw looking back at me had become the very father figure he was searching for his whole life.

I never would have learned that had it not been for Dr. Kelly, my wife Teresa, my daughters Jordan and Alexis, my son Devon, my mom Gwen, my niece Geri and her kids and all the other people who supported me through the years.

I wear my heart on my sleeve so what you see, is what you get.

I'm a better man because of them and the work that I did in therapy.

I made a lot of progress on my journey to heal and I'm still working at it. I enjoy the quality of life that I dreamed of as a kid. I am strong. I am wise. I believe in letting my light shine. I am worth it and I deserve it.

I learned how to communicate better and I finally feel safe in my own skin. I am so thankful for the life that I live and would gladly go through all of it again just to get to where I am now. I am good to go but I will continue to work on myself to be better.

And I know exactly who I am.

I am Resilient!

Acknowledgments

Dear Lord, thank you for blessing me since before I was even born. Please continue to give me clarity and the awareness of your blessings as they pass in front of me so I can do something productive with them to better my life and those around me. Please continue to allow me to be a beacon of light for others.

Teresa, you are my wife and guardian angel, and I love you more than you will ever know. Thank you for being with me all these years. Thank you for lifting me up in a way that no one else could. You are the most intelligent and nicest person I have ever met.

To my daughters Jordan and Alexis, you two are incredibly strong yet sensitive women. I love that you have that balance in you. I love you and I love watching you grow and learn about life. You are resilient too and I am always cheering for you. To my mother Gwen, you were right there by my side doing the best you could, and it was enough for me. Thank you for never letting me down in this lifetime. You have always been there for me, and I will always be here for you. I am so happy and blessed to call you mom. I love you very much and I am still trying to make you proud. To my niece Geri, our talks have always made me feel better. You have great energy and it's been amazing watching you grow into the woman that you are. You have a heart of gold and I have witnessed your faith and how you bless others with your time and love. You have raised 5 amazing young people. Kamrynn, McKenzie, Jameson, Payton and Aubrey, I love you guys. Thank you to Michael Rubin, you have always been a loyal friend and I have personally witnessed your generosity towards our childhood friends and many others. You have been authentic from the start. Keep up the great work you do in the world and like you always say… "We are just getting started!" Love you buddy and I will always have your back.

To my friend Richard Lawson, thank you for being my TV dad. Someone that I could emulate. A black man who showed the world intelligence, class, pride and talent. In real life, it's been a pleasure getting to know you and not just your character Nick Kimball. You are a great and generous man and I'm glad you survived that deadly New York plane crash in 1992. To Altura (Darth Vader) Ewers, It's always good to see you buddy. You have always been a good friend. A huge thank you to Kevin Dale for your guidance. Your words of wisdom have served me well and I'd have a cigar with you anywhere in the world buddy. Thanks to Greg Moore, you are a brilliant man and I appreciate your comments prompting me to include a preface in my book. I'd like to thank my entire family and all of my childhood friends for your respect, friendship, love and support. I appreciate you for helping to create my life experiences both good and bad.

Much love to everyone born and raised in Norristown, "You already know, you are not what the world says you are, you are what you say you are." To George and Linda Harrison, you showed me what black excellence was before it was a thing. Also, you raised a loving, kind and intelligent son that I call a friend. Thanks to Cory Hott and Hadley Passela of Hott + Hadley Writing Consultancy. You two have been there every step of the way guiding me on this literary project and I can't thank you enough. Thanks to my friend George Beach for always cheering for me. I would like to send a special shout out and a huge thank you to musician and businessman, Trey Songz. We just happened to sit next to each other on a plane leaving Atlanta and coming home to LA. I was working on this book and then we got to talking for the next 3 hours. He was very nice to me and the conversation was meaningful. I left the plane but forgot my computer in the pocket of the seat in front of me. As I was walking, I heard someone yelling my name, so I turned around as he was bringing my laptop to me on the jetway. I didn't have it backed up at the time so that would have been a nightmare for me and set me way back on its completion.

And lastly, to my son Devon. I love you and want the best for you and your son. I look forward to reconnecting with you one of these days after you heal and get your life in order. Teresa and I will always be here to offer love, guidance and support but we have boundaries that need to be respected. Life can be a beautiful thing and I don't want you and your son to miss out. Time goes by so quickly and before we know it, we have grays and wrinkles and then we are gone. Don't let time get the better of you. Do the right thing, the right way, until you get the right results.

About the Author

Lenny is a husband, father, friend and author. He has a fine art degree and is a serial entrepreneur who has conceptualized and created 12 different start-ups. He is an angel investor in multiple ventures as well as an equity investor in a major software company. He is the Co-Associate Executive Producer on the new TV show, Beyond Black (A Supernatural Political Thriller.) He loves making short films and being around film in general. He is an artist who paints and generally creates and while on a trip to China in 2012, he consulted with a Feng Shui Master, who taught him simple principles based on color, material and placement.

This is where he picked up his nickname, Zen Len. He uses the learned design principles in his art and construction projects as a real estate developer in Los Angeles. He is also the Life Coach for the LA Trade Tech Men's College Basketball Team. In 2023, he was inducted into the Norristown Area High School Hall of Fame but not for his football talent. It was in recognition of his philanthropy.

Teresa and I in Antarctica

My mom Gwen and step dad JB

My dad Hampton Coleman Jr. on the right and my high school
track coach Ernie Hadrick Jr.

4 year old me and my half sister Tara

My cousin Nimmy

Little league baseball with Nike sneakers

1st year playing on the Cardinals

Me and Michael Rubin at the Sixers game

Me at 28 years old with my 3 kids

Me and the kids

Me and my "As seen on TV" dad Richard Lawson

1980's Pepsi & NFL bottle cap
marketing challenge

www.ingramcontent.com/pod-product-compliance
Lightning Source LLC
Chambersburg PA
CBHW020238130626
46549CB00005B/1955